THE DISTRACTION-PROOF ADVISOR

THE DISTRACTION-**PROOF** ADVISOR

Gain Control, Work Smarter, Succeed Sooner

PAUL KINGSMAN

Published by Focused Potential
www.FocusedPotential.com

ISBN 978-0-9962261-0-3

Project Consultant: Cynthia A. Zigmund of Second City Publishing Services LLC

Cover and Interior Design: Summer R. Morris of Sumo Design Studio

Editor: Jack Kiburz

Printed in the United States of America.

This book is dedicated to Aliesha and Jack—
thanks for always believing!

CONTENTS

INTRODUCTION
SIMPLE DOESN'T MEAN EASY!

"There are no easy answers—but there are simple answers."

– RONALD REAGAN, ACTOR, POLITICIAN,
40TH PRESIDENT OF THE UNITED STATES

Winning an Olympic medal is simple. In fact, it's a lot like building a great financial services business:

- Consider what you want to achieve.

- Realistically assess your present situation.

- Set a deadline for accomplishing your objective.

- Be passionate about achieving your desired outcome.

- Have a clear vision of what success will be like.

- Learn the actions to take.

- Create a plan with a time line.

- Take the actions.

- Succeed!

It's very straightforward. The steps are clear.

At this point, you're probably wondering, "If it is that easy, why don't more advisors have the thriving businesses they want? Why don't *I* have the thriving business *I* want? Why isn't it that *easy* for me?"

This is where frustration begins for many advisors. Notice I didn't say it was *easy*—I only said it was *simple!* We can quickly, and wrongly, assume that if something is simple—that is, if it's plainly and clearly understood—then it should require little effort to accomplish. In other words, it should be *easy*. However, just because something is simple to understand doesn't mean it is easy to do. Easy sounds so appealing that—when it comes to success—people waste a lot of time looking for nonexistent quick and easy ways to the top, instead of using that time and effort to simply take the steps needed to achieve their dreams.

The distilled nature of today's information makes us particularly vulnerable to this trap of confusing *easy* with *simple:* we expect the most important points to come in infographics, bullet points, or at least fewer than 140 characters. When the directions and objectives are so simply stated and come at us so quickly, we can erroneously expect the results, or output, to come just as fast, with as little effort as it took for us to receive and process the input. Then, when we don't instantaneously achieve the success we want, we're left frustrated.

Think about how many times you've thought about (or tried) losing weight or heard about others attempting to do so. The process for losing weight is simple: expend more calories than you consume. However, people spend big bucks to get help with this simple process because it is tough to do. The US weight-loss market now exceeds $60 billion and is expected to continue growing![1] This huge industry exists to help people lose weight because shedding extra pounds, while simple, is not easy. In the same way that losing weight is simple but not easy, building a great financial services business is not complicated, but it's also not easy.

While there are some advisors who need direction to identify what to do to build a business, it's likely that you are among the many more who already know what it takes. You know you need to find centers of influence, continue hunting for solid relationships with your ideal target clients, prospect, ask for referrals, move from a transactional to a fee-based business, segment your book, and time-block. The problem isn't knowing what to do (that's simple); the problem is managing to get all those activities done. That's not easy!

There are emails to answer, phone calls to make, reports to read, colleagues to consult, meetings to attend, strategies to plan and monitor, investments to track and analyze, employees to manage, and on and on— all while you're trying to build and run a business! It's common to address the most urgent demands at the expense of the most important needs. After all the frantic bouncing around from one demanding activity to the next, you're tired and feel like you're not making much progress toward the original dream you had when you first began in this business. In short, you are distracted from doing the *best* things to move your business toward your vision.

You are not alone. A Financial Planning Association Research and Practice Institute study revealed that more than half of the advisors surveyed said they were not in control of their time, with 49 percent claiming they were not in control of their businesses.[2] Only 10 percent felt in complete control of their businesses. Those advisors studied diligently to pass arduous exams, so they were clearly serious about their profession, but an extraordinarily high percentage of them still felt frustrated, overwhelmed, and out of control in regards to their businesses.

LOOKING FOR CONTROL OF YOUR BUSINESS LIFE

When our experience becomes overwhelming rather than idyllic, we understandably start searching for new methods, innovative approaches, and secret formulas. We fervently search for insights into how to imitate the success of the 10 percent of advisors who do feel in complete control of their businesses.

I witnessed this in my swimming career. When I was just breaking into the international swimming ranks, many New Zealand coaches were unduly enamored with training techniques used by Australian and American coaches, believing they had the "secrets" that would propel swimmers to success. These New Zealand coaches frequently changed their swimmers' drills and exercises based on the latest information about what coaches were doing overseas. Some would change their programs so frequently that swimmers never had time to experience the benefits from any one particular approach before they moved on to the next. They spent a lot of energy learning and implementing novel ways to do things, but the swimmers made few measurable improvements in their performances. While my coach and I kept informed about new techniques others were using, we focused on a core group of exercises we believed would prepare me to compete successfully. We rarely made changes to the techniques we had chosen to concentrate on, and when we did, it was for a deliberate reason. Keep in mind that "new and different" may just be new and different and not necessarily better or improved.

Many advisors who have sought coaching from me have initially thought the solution to attaining the success they wanted lay in developing a better vision for their business. In reality, though, most advisors already had a great vision for what they wanted from the time they entered the industry, but that vision had been buried under their growing "busyness." As we worked together, they rediscovered that original picture of what they wanted. They remembered the initial dreams that ignited their passion and their vivid image of working with wonderful, thrilled clients while managing the onslaught of great referrals. They recalled the picture of enjoying relaxing time with their families, secure in knowing they had built a solid fee-based business that kept generating cash flow and provided them with the freedom to do what they wanted. But soon after getting started, they got swamped. They kept working harder and doing more to achieve a dream that seemed increasingly elusive and soon out of sight altogether, causing their frustration to grow. Remembering that original vision provided some help, but it was just the first step to finding the solution they were really searching for.

Many advisors seek to address their vexation about vision by working on their goals. They admit to being distracted and want help identifying the "right" goals that will move them toward their vision. Ironically, having specific goals clearly identified can actually increase your frustration. These days, most of us are pretty good at setting goals. We probably learned to do it in school, from managers who expected written goals from us at the end of each year, and in business-building literature that constantly encouraged us to identify our objectives. The question is, Is it working? Is your list of goals bringing you the relief and results you want?

DREAM + GOAL + DISTRACTION = FRUSTRATION

As a young age-group swimmer, I trained with several kids who were very talented athletes. They were good swimmers and talented tennis players and strong cyclists and excellent rugby players. They had plenty of dreams and goals of excelling in every sport they played. But ultimately, their broad range of activities was their undoing: they were constantly distracted from concentrating on and mastering any one sport and so made very little progress in any of their activities. They became discouraged when they began to regularly lose to other, more focused competitors.

It's no different in our grown-up world of business. Setting goals is important. Having distilled our objectives into pithy bullet points, we can see exactly where we want to go. But then we get deluged with distractions: there is always just too much to do and our destination seems forever out of reach. All the while, we expend more and more of our finite energy and emotions, only making those goals seem even more elusive. At the end of the day, we still have our lists, but we're not making the progress we want, and now we're frustrated and tired.

When advisors realize their vision and goals haven't brought the calm and contentment they're seeking, the next stage many go through is thinking they need more information about how to operate in this industry. But this drive to learn more raises another frustrating roadblock, as more articles, ideas, and opinions specifically relevant to our industry are available than ever before. From *Investment Advisor* to *Financial Planning* to *REP* to *On Wall Street* to LinkedIn groups to blogs and so many more outlets, each article brings new ideas, interesting commentary, helpful feedback, and examples of things to try, activities to do, and trouble to avoid. With so many great resources available from tenured industry specialists, it would seem that advisors should all be flying toward their magical AUM (assets under management) numbers—the ones we first wrote down when we were encouraged to dream big at our company training programs immediately after passing our licensing exams. Alas, that's just not the case. Instead, we often find ourselves overwhelmed with information, and if we're not paralyzed by it we end up running ourselves ragged, flitting from one activity to another, hoping each successive one will bring the elusive success we long for. You may find yourself repeatedly back at the point of that frantic bouncing around from activity to activity, rarely getting the very important things done, and secretly wondering if you really have what it takes to make it in this business.

HOW TO BREAK THE CYCLE OF DISTRACTIONS

There is a way out of this exasperating cycle! You can build a great business, make a decent living with clients you actually want to work with, and have more control of your time. Your frustration is treatable and beatable. You can gain control of your focus and energy so that you can achieve success. You can learn how to earn the right to expect success, all the time, whether attracting prospects, structuring your business, or presenting to clients. You can achieve outstanding results. But first, you need to understand the distractions that are creating the obstacles that keep you from your desired destination.

What do these distractions look like and what will it take to overcome them? It would be great to have a guide every step of the way—someone who knows how it feels to prospect and grow your business while tracking incoming ACATs; someone who understands your desire to pursue larger, more profitable clients and still tend to the administrative details for smaller clients who rely on you to play a vital role in their financial lives; someone who has experienced the aggravation of developing an ideal business process with specific steps to take but has been continually bogged down in minutiae.

Look no further! Having worked in the industry since 2001, I get it. I also know the mindset, habits, and persistence needed to succeed aren't secrets; I've used them myself as an Olympic medalist and as a financial advisor, and I've taught them to advisors as a speaker and consultant. I know the everyday challenges you face, and what it's like to want to break free from the frustrations and distractions that hold you back from what you want. I've written this book to share my experiences with you and help you achieve your own dreams.

This book is not an exhaustive step-by-step guide to structuring a financial services business. For something like that, I'd suggest you get a copy of Deena Katz's excellent book *On Practice Management*. Ron Carson's and Steve Sanduski's *Tested in the Trenches* is also a good resource for this, especially for teams.

This book is for advisors who find themselves distracted and want to know how to refocus on the key, core basics of finding new prospects and engaging them in compelling and realistic dialogue to turn them into great clients.

It's also for new (and not-so-new) advisors who feel daunted by all there is to do to succeed in this industry. This book will help you understand the critical habits you need to develop and the approaches you need to consistently adopt if you want to reach your objectives sooner.

This book is for independent advisors who can feel isolated—those who want some direction, fresh ideas, and confirmation regarding what they are doing to help them maintain their motivation and conviction.

Finally, this book is also for seasoned advisors who may be looking to bring on junior partners and want to help them quickly develop a sound approach and solid structure to effectively grow their business.

We'll walk through how to create a plan that fits you, determine a process that works for you, and establish a system to keep you accountable so you can get where you want to go. We will go beyond the simple steps of *what* you need to do so you will learn *how* to apply the business-building steps to your own unique situation and objectives.

If you still want to achieve that initial vision you had when you first got started in this business, this book is for you. If you've kept that vision alive or want to reignite it, this book is for you. This book is especially for you if you desperately want to structure your time and focus your energy to overcome deadly distractions and realize your desire to have a thriving, fun business.

First, let's let go of the ideas of "easy" and "hard"—they're relative. People often think my training for an Olympic medal was hard, yet for me, while definitely challenging, it was not hard. Being blind and climbing Mt. Everest sounds hard to me, but people who have done it say it's not: you just keep putting one foot in front of the other and hold on tightly. Building a great business is not necessarily easy or hard, but it does require commitment, tenacity, and focus. Those words don't hold a lot of attraction for many people today, but they are the foundation to building a great business and living a contented, rather than frustrating, life. It will be work, and it will definitely keep you busy, but it'll be that good, productive, solid busy that brings positive results.

In spite of what you may have heard before, there simply aren't any mysterious formulas for success, so there is no need to keep searching for some magic secrets. Bringing your vision of your business to reality is possible, and as I've said, it is simple, which means you won't have to bend your mind to figure it out. You'll understand the vital attitudes and critical activities needed to succeed, and you'll also learn to recognize destructive thought patterns and damaging habits to avoid. We will address daily steps that will lead to the business success you want.

We'll begin by uncovering the distractions you will fall into if you are not clear about *why* you're doing what you're doing. Then you'll see why being specific is so important to your success, and you'll learn an effective, measurable way to record your objectives to provide yourself with accountability. We'll look at conviction and why you need it (not the SEC kind of conviction you don't want, but the deep conviction that's necessary to overcome the myriad mind games you'll permit if you waver at this point). We'll review wording to use for effective dialogues at various points in your process. We'll cover the important tool of time-blocking, and why, if you don't use it in this industry, you'll be swamped.

Each chapter opens with a list of distractions advisors face if they don't employ the simple steps and approaches outlined. These are real challenges that real advisors (both clients and colleagues) have raised in our conversations together. As a producing advisor, I still face these distractions myself. If you find the distractions dominating your current situation, don't worry; keep reading to learn the prescription to overcome them and get back on track.

KNOWING VERSUS BELIEVING

We've covered the vital difference between simple and easy and should no longer be concerning ourselves about whether actions seem easy or hard. Yet, there still is one more critical differentiation to clarify before we dive in: Don't confuse *knowing* with *believing*.

We have access to more information today than we'll ever need, yet there have never been more people who struggle to stay committed or to deeply, truly believe in themselves and what they can achieve. We are overflowing with knowledge, yet we have less confidence in what we know.

As I mentioned, most advisors know what to do to build a great business but find it difficult to believe it enough to respond every day by eradicating distractions and remaining committed to doing the best things. Do you *believe* you can build the business you want? Have you developed your vision for your business until you can see it in 3-D and then let it settle into your heart and take root in your mind? Have you nurtured that vision to become more than just something you know and let it become something you truly believe in?

Your belief needs to evolve into conviction, and your conviction will spur you to action. My weight-training coach, Don Oliver, was a fierce weight lifter in his day. He would always say that he would much rather face a lifter with twice his ability who doubted himself, than a guy with half his ability who believed he could win. "They're the dangerous ones," he told me. The people who may not have everything together yet, but who know they are heading in the right direction and believe it is only a matter of time until everything clicks into place, are the people who go on to do great things.

I adopted that approach in my Olympic medal pursuit. I had to; I wasn't born with an outstanding physique for a swimmer. At 6 feet, I'm not particularly tall; I don't have arms with an albatross-like span to pull me through the water; and my size-11 feet aren't big enough to be amazing flippers. Those with "natural ability" still have to work for what they want, but even though I didn't have the innate physical characteristics to give me an edge, I refused to let that hold me back. I developed a vision I firmly believed in. I knew if I applied myself rigorously to a routine that made sense to me, one day I'd have a shot at measuring myself against the greatest swimmers in the world. By staying focused and paying attention to vital details, I hit my target and won a medal.

The process successful athletes use to reach their goals is the same method needed to create wildly successful financial services businesses.

They're not for a lucky few with unusual natural abilities—they are available to everyone!

So, do *you* believe in your vision of your business enough to make it a reality? If you're serious about gaining control, working smarter, and succeeding sooner, and if you're prepared to do what it takes, join me and read on.

CHAPTER ONE

KNOW WHY YOU'RE IN THIS BUSINESS

*"Dream up the kind of world you want to live in—
dream out loud—at high volume."*

– BONO, ROCK BAND U2 LEAD SINGER, SONGWRITER,
AND SOCIAL JUSTICE CRUSADER

If you are not clear about what you want from your business, you'll be distracted by any or all of the following:

- New ideas

- Self-doubt

- Client requests

- Responding more than planning

- Servicing nonideal clients

Great results don't just happen. They are a culmination of detailed, consistent, honest, focused planning and actions, directed toward a very clear objective. This chapter will help you understand why you need to know what you want from your business and why you must believe you can get it.

From the moment you started in this industry, you likely had a client quota to fill—you spoke to anyone who had a pulse and signed up people like your Uncle Bill with his "massive" $53,589 IRA rollover. ("There's another five-grand where that came from if you do well!") That's okay. Everyone needs to begin somewhere, and these family accounts may have kept you motivated when you were just getting started, learning important things about the industry and yourself as you gained experience.

As your AUM grew, your confidence increased. You met more people and even considered adhering to a process (if you found one you were comfortable with). You began to catch a glimpse of what could be—of what you might be able to create for yourself and your clients. You started to feel more certain about what you were doing and how you were doing it, and you began looking forward to more opportunities coming your way. Your determination strengthened with successes and as you considered what further steps to take to build your dreams.

Then it hit: You started to feel frazzled by everything you had to do each day. You may still have caught glimpses of that grand vision in your mind, but you began to be more focused on the immediacy of issues around you. You found yourself pulled in many different directions, constantly needing to tend to small, yet urgent issues as you serviced your initial clients.

You knew you wanted to spend more time and energy finding larger clients, growing your business, and fine-tuning your process, but you were distracted from these activities by the daily "busyness" of running your business. You read articles about centers of influence, niche strategies, and ideal clients, and yearned for the day when you would finally arrive at "that place."

Arrive where? By when? How? At what cost?

Several years ago I received an email from a prospective coaching client. When I visited her website, it was difficult to determine what specific expertise she offered her own clients. She listed a broad range of client scenarios and was basically trying to communicate that she could help anyone with any financial advisory need, from employees with stock options, to firms with 401(k) plans, to executives considering retirement. When we eventually spoke, I wasn't surprised to hear that Cheryl was feeling overwhelmed. She bemoaned the fact that there was simply too much to keep up with regarding all the different areas she was trying to cover.

While I believe there are merits to taking a broader approach to building your business rather than strictly limiting yourself to a very narrow niche group, I asked Cheryl to distill her approach and name what her ultimate objective was when she started in this business. Like many advisors I talk with, she told me it was to help people plan best for their financial future. From there we explored her personal financial goals for her business, what types of clients she most wanted to help, and what kind of guidance she could provide. Once she was able to clearly communicate what she wanted to do and who she wanted to do it for, she could spot busy activities that were actually distractions to avoid.

Without clear answers in your mind and heart about where you want to go, how you plan to get there, and when you plan to arrive, distractions will pull you away from your big vision as they creep in and start taking over. If you can articulate the answers to questions about what your business will look like, you will begin to see how it fits into your life, when it is going to happen, and how you're going to do it. Once you know these specifics, record them where you can constantly see them. We'll talk about that in the next chapter, but for now let's look at how those distractions happen.

UNDERSTAND THE "WHY" IN WHAT YOU DO

The most successful people know exactly *why* they do specific tasks. They keep their long-term objective clearly in mind, relating to it on a daily basis. They don't get distracted. They are resolute about where they are going, know how to get there, and are committed to taking the steps that get them there soonest. Nothing is permitted to get in their way, douse their desire, or prevent them from reaching what they know they can achieve. They are accomplished at what they do, but more important, they carry a deep understanding about *why* they do it and where it fits in their grand plan for their lives.

Do you have a sense of "why" regarding what you're doing? Is it as strong as it was when you first began building your business?

There's a lot of pressure in this industry to identify *what* you will do as an advisor. When you're a new advisor, there are regular benchmarks to hit or you face losing your job. More years in the industry bring more experience, with quarterly and annual goals and reviews with managers. These goals always involve doing more—acquiring *more* assets, securing *more* clients, establishing *more* contacts, being *more* productive, providing *more* service. You may become so used to looking for the next big milestone that you get caught up in the process of desiring and producing more as an end in itself. Because there are so many external pressures from managers, the media, and our culture to do and have more, it can seem like it is unquestionably the only way to get what you want. Growth can seem like the best and ultimate goal.

Often the picture that develops equates personal success with *doing* things—the more you are doing, the more successful you are. You may envision yourself *doing* business building, *doing* client relationships and service, *doing* planning, even *doing* family relationships, friendships, and community service, all with efficiency, speed, grace, and style. If you can only successfully *do* all the things on your to-do list, then you'll *be* successful. When you're in this mindset, success means *do more*.

The problem is that there always remains more to do, and success becomes even more elusive. Getting on a "more, more, more" treadmill produces a lot of activity but often little substance or contentment. This can leave you feeling like you're not really going anywhere, and the success you want so badly seems forever out of reach in an overpacked life. So, how do you get off the treadmill and actually go somewhere?

After almost 20 years in the industry, a seasoned advisor I worked with made a decision not to seek new clients. He had examined what he wanted from his business—his revenue goals, the types of clients he wanted to work with, and the time to enjoy the lifestyle he wanted—and realized he had accomplished what he set out to achieve. He knew he could make more money if he continued driving to build his business, but he decided he didn't want to do the work it would require to develop new prospects. He greatly enjoyed his relationships with his clients and his work for them and decided to focus on cultivating and deepening those existing bonds. One of his goals was to meet the children of his top-tier clients to assist with wealth transition plans and eventually explore how he could help them with assets they had. He was content to strengthen his business in this way and not continually strive and actively market for more clients.

While having goals to grow what you already have can be good, before turning our attention to what you're going to do and achieve, let's step out of the mindset of always needing to do more and consider *why* you're doing what you do. *Why* do you want more assets? *Why* do you want more clients? *Why* are you building your business? In short, what will be the resulting benefits that make your diligent work worth it? Daily task lists can keep you busy, but remember where we started: Building a great financial services business is simple, but it's not easy. What motivates you to stay connected with your clients, even when the market takes a downturn? What is really important to *you*?

Many of the techniques competitive athletes use to hone their skills and sharpen their focus can be highly applicable and useful in your business efforts. Visualizing is an important tool for athletes, and in the Introduction I encouraged you to develop a vivid, 3-D vision of what you want, imagining how it will look and feel. Typically, athletes have a big advantage when it comes to visualizing: they can easily watch others perform at high levels and readily see their focus, attention, and persistence. They can observe actions that cause disappointing defeat and study those that bring exhilarating success. Every day, athletes learn and benefit from others who have accomplished more as they improve themselves. By doing this, they equip themselves to tolerate short-term discomfort, knowing that if they persevere, like those they are emulating have done, success can be theirs, too. Watching others perform like they aspire to do fuels athletes' visions and keeps them motivated.

When I was preparing for my first Olympics I practically wore out a videotape called *The Fast and the Furious*. It profiled Alex Bauman and Victor Davis, two Canadian swimmers who were relentless in their drive for excellence and swimming as fast as possible. They were tough and didn't let adversity hold them back from achieving world records. I watched how they practiced and listened as they expressed their thoughts about training and their racing rationale. I studied how they mentally processed their experiences and learned from their approaches and mindsets. Watching them greatly influenced how I pursued my own swimming goals.

As advisors, we often don't get to see the step-by-step, daily actions that go into building a successful business. There are very few insightful, riveting documentaries about financial advisors and how they achieved their success! We may hear stories about risks taken and profitable outcomes, or read biographical accounts *after* a person has become hugely successful, but we typically don't readily get to witness how everything unfolds in another advisor's business, seeing how they handle setbacks, regroup, and bounce back along the way. But gaining valuable insights into how others have succeeded and using their experiences to shorten your own learning curve are good strategies. Look for a mentor. It is easier than you think; most people are kind and willing to give help to someone who directly asks. One way you can find potential mentors is to review the lists of larger successful advisors that industry magazines publish each year—or advisors who are the focus of profile articles— and select a few to research. Email one or two advisors who particularly interest you, congratulate them on being featured in the magazine, let them know you were inspired or motivated by what they did or said, and ask for 20 minutes of their time over the phone. Briefly let them know where you are in your career and tell them you understand they're busy and that you value their time. Offer to email four or five questions to them and then set up a phone appointment within the next two weeks to hear and discuss their responses. If they do grant you an interview, be respectful of their time and keep the call to the agreed 20 minutes. Send them a handwritten thank-you note immediately after the call and express your appreciation for their time and insights. You may develop relationships with a couple of mentors you can reconnect with and seek counsel from when you face challenges as your own business grows. Also, working with a coach who is a specialist in the industry and has insights into how advisors run their businesses can be very helpful.

Spend deliberate time thinking about the desired results of your hard work and nurturing a clear picture of your success. Perhaps you want to generate enough money in fees so that you are free to spend a long weekend away with your spouse once a quarter to reconnect and deepen your relationship. What will be the benefits from tending to this important area of your life? Or maybe you want to take your entire family on a dream vacation. What lasting memories do you want to make? As your child leaves for college, what will it be like to experience the assurance of your rock-solid relationship because of the specific, special times you carved out as a parent? You might want to earn enough money to give away 20 percent of your gross income to support the charitable work of two causes you believe in. How will you feel knowing you helped to equip others to live better lives? Maybe you'd like to take off one afternoon each week to coach your child's soccer team, secure in knowing that the business you generate at other times is sufficient to allow you that flexibility in your work schedule.

One of my priorities when our son was a preschooler was to have the freedom to be at home with him during the day. I structured my business activities to allow time for this. Though our son is now in his 20s, he and I still talk and laugh about our memories from those days. Now, I make it a priority in my schedule each week to do chaplaincy work, leading Bible studies with inmates at our local jail.

Identifying the specific benefits of your hard work can be an easy step to skip. In fact, some of you might be tempted to start skimming these pages now in order to get to the "action steps" in the book. While I appreciate your eagerness, I encourage you to slow down and take the time to deliberately develop your image of success. Think about the perks you will enjoy. Let your imagination run and picture your life the way you want it to be. Go beyond crossing off items on a to-do list. Taking the time to invest in this step now will make the later steps in our process together much more effective!

Nurturing this picture of what the end point of your diligent work will look and feel like is the most effective way to develop a deep conviction for what you're doing and motivate yourself on this journey. Top athletes begin their day with their image in mind, using it to keep them on track when things get difficult. They often end their day exhausted, and sometimes frustrated, yet in those final moments of the evening that image is the last thought on their mind as they drift to sleep and rest for the next day of their pursuit.

When I was training for the Olympics, I had a photo of an Olympic medal pasted in the front of my training log book. Each day, after I finished recording the details of that day's workout, I turned to the inside front cover and looked at that medal. It reminded me of where I was heading and helped me refocus. On tough days when I was sore and tired and things had not gone as well as I had hoped, it helped me remember why I was working so hard and sacrificing so much. I longed to experience the thrill of winning and anticipated the sensations that would come with achieving my long-term goal. Keeping my ideal outcome fresh in my mind and heart assured me each day that the cost I was paying was worth it.

When I got home at night, I took imaging a step further. As I sat by myself in my family's spa pool, soothing my aching muscles and trying to soak out the chlorine that burned my skin, I rehearsed the script for my imagined role as a famous Olympic medalist starring in a milk commercial. The benefits of achieving my goal became so tangible that the immediate discomfort of the training faded to a mere detail; aching muscles and chlorine-burned skin were just necessary steps along the journey to the success that I was confident would eventually happen.

Seeing where your diligent work could lead you is vital. Keep a palpable representation of it in front of you. Whether you have a photo montage of your family on vacation on your refrigerator or a picture of people from a developing nation for whom you will fund an irrigation project posted by your computer, you must have a way of keeping your mission, vision, and values clearly in sight. Make the time and create the opportunity to see that picture every day.

My goal for the Olympics was to swim the 200-meter backstroke in two minutes; my coach and I believed that would be fast enough to win a medal. To help me stay focused while I was training, one afternoon my coach took a ladder, climbed up to each of the two analog pace clocks mounted on the walls at either end of the pool, and painted a blue stripe on the top of the clock at the 60-second mark. Every time I pushed off either wall of the pool, I saw a reminder of what I was striving for. Two minutes became embedded in my mind. Although I had never swum that fast before, the thought of successfully hitting that time was reinforced with each lap. Because I was constantly focused on that time, achieving it seemed inevitable—more a matter of simply needing to formalize it, rather than it being a daunting trial.

PICTURE YOUR DREAM

Now that my days of being a sports celebrity are behind me, my dreams are different. Every few years I like to take the time to create a montage (some people call it a dream board) of what the business success I desire now will allow me to do. I take pictures of the people and organizations I want to support, of places I want to visit, and of my family as we enjoy time together, and scan them to make wallpaper for my computer. The freedom to do and enjoy these things is why I work hard, and seeing these images each day keeps me motivated for the work I have to do. (See Figure 1.1 for an example of one of my own dream board montages from a few years ago.) I pray that God will show me whether my plans line up with His and then begin moving forward to the next step.

Figure 1.1 My Dream Board

There are lots of ways to develop your own picture; your approach will depend on your personality. I respond strongly to sensory input, so I like to imagine the vivid colors, the sounds, the smells, the looks of people's expressions, and the emotions I will feel when I achieve my goal and am enjoying the benefits of what I've accomplished. Maybe you're more analytical and prefer to imagine a plan about things you will do on a trip, how a conversation with a loved one will unfold, or steps you will take to learn a new skill. Whatever your approach, get off that demanding treadmill to *do* more and pause to think about what you want and why. This short-term effort is more than feel-good fluff; it is a crucial foundational step in progressing toward your success.

You might need to stop reading at this point and take time to think for a day or two—mute the music during your commute, shut down the computer, leave the TV off. Make some quiet time and space to really think. What will the success you want look like? Specifically name the benefits you'll enjoy once you've achieved that success.

Having a literal picture of what your success will look like will make the later work feel more manageable. Distractions will become more obvious, and you'll be less willing to justify those things that suck up your time but don't move you forward. Focusing your efforts on doing the most valuable things is much more feasible when you have a clear vision of the rewards.

Once you have identified those benefits you want to enjoy, we'll move to the next chapter and get started on how you're going to attain them and make your life better, not just busier.

DEVELOP A VIVID PICTURE
OF YOUR DREAM

Cultivate your picture of what your diligent work will lead to. Clarify what you want. Create statements in the first person and in the present tense. Use the questions below to generate ideas to help you get specific about your "why."

- Imagine your perfect day.
  - Where are you?
  - What are you doing?
  - Who are you with?
  - How does this make you feel?
  - What energizes and excites you?

- Who do you want to be?
  - How is your physical life?
  - What positive emotions do you typically feel?
  - Where are you spiritually?

- What are your relationships like—with colleagues, clients, friends, and family?
  - What do you believe in?
  - What do you stand for?
  - How are you impacting the lives of others?
  - How do those who know you best describe you?

- What do you want to have?
  - What does having that allow you to do?
  - How does having that make you feel?

DISTRACTION-PROOF STEPS

1. Be clear about why you're doing what you're doing.

2. Make time to record your vision in writing or visually.

3. Keep a clear picture of your goals on your mind to keep you pointed where you want to go.

Borrow the athlete's method of holding your picture of success tightly in your mind, using it to keep you moving forward in the face of challenging circumstances. Keeping that image vivid and prominent will increase your awareness of ways to overcome distractions that may be interesting but irrelevant.

Now that you have your clear picture in mind, let's begin to format it so you can track your progress toward it.

CHAPTER TWO
TARGET YOUR GOALS

"If you don't know where you are going,
you'll end up someplace else."

– YOGI BERRA, MAJOR LEAGUE BASEBALL PLAYER,
COACH, AND MANAGER

I f you are vague about when you will achieve your objective, you will fail to hold yourself accountable for doing what matters most and become distracted by:

- Unsuitable prospects who waste your time

- Unimportant actions that drain your energy, leaving you lacking the vitality needed to accomplish crucial activities

- Dreaming about what could be, instead of taking definitive steps to make it happen

- Every new idea about how to build your business

Successful advisors hold themselves accountable. They recognize their actions will either cause them to arrive at their destination sooner or waste energy prolonging their journey and diminishing their chances of success. Thoughts alone—even great thoughts—are not enough to bring the rewards you desire.

MAKING THINGS HAPPEN

You have already done the powerful work of developing your vivid picture of what success looks like, and you know *why* you want a thriving business. Now you are prepared to start identifying explicit checkpoints so you can track your progress as you move along your path to reach the success you want.

Statements like, "I want to build a thriving business with clients I like and who appreciate what I do" or, "I want to help people be financially free" are too vague. To build a viable business, first determine what revenue you need to keep your doors open and how much time you have to create that income. "I want to grow my business" is another vague goal I've often heard stated. Do you mean you want to grow your income, expand your number of clients, or increase your number of employees? What do you want to grow to? Some advisors say they want to develop more referral relationships with complementary professionals. That is a good element to factor into your overall business growth strategy, but again, it's not specific enough. Who do you want to cultivate relationships with—CPAs, estate attorneys, divorce attorneys? How many of these relationships do you want?

Without being more specific, there is little for you to track and no realistic way to hold yourself accountable for making progress toward enjoying the benefits you identified in Chapter 1. Getting detailed and precise will help you avoid the distractions that constantly threaten to derail you. Determine the crucial steps you need to take, so you do not end up just dreaming about what could be and fool yourself into thinking that one day you'll eventually get there.

This means we're back to picture building, but this time it's about what your practice will look like when you have the thriving business you want. Who is your ideal client? What level of assets do you want under management? What will you do, and what will associates or support staff do? When are you going to accomplish these things? Decide how you're getting to where you're going and, importantly, when you'll get there.

Most people aren't specific enough about their goals because they're afraid they won't achieve them. They think saying they want to grow their assets is enough—justifying their not naming a certain number by claiming they don't want to limit themselves to some arbitrary figure. The truth is, most people simply want to avoid the disappointment of not achieving what they hoped for. They are already too focused on what might happen if they miss their goal. Others may feel they are being thorough enough by including a specific measure of progress—grow AUM by 10 percent, for instance. While this is an important element, it doesn't effectively complete the goal-setting process.

When you were going through the licensing process, you had to be specific. You had a definite date when you would take your exam and knew you needed to study to master the precise material on which you would be tested. The deadline of your test date forced you to focus and judiciously allocate your time so you could be prepared to pass. When I was studying for my initial advisory licenses and later professional accreditations, I fell back on the training routine I developed when I swam of getting up early and working while most people were still asleep.

Many advisors seek the support of their family and friends, who for a short while stop expecting them to participate in evening or weekend activities, allowing them uninterrupted time to study. That test date influenced my thoughts, focus, and effort, as I'm sure it did for you. Because you couldn't begin your career without the requisite licenses, you pushed through the tasks and reached your objective. That kind of precise concentration and application will help you set your specific goals to continue forward.

If you read the introduction to this book, you might remember my saying that setting specific goals increases frustration levels and wonder why I'm now recommending setting clearly defined objectives. Most of our business process planning starts *and ends* with setting goals. If all you do with your goals is use them to make a list of wishes or activities and then file them away, never looking at them again until the next time someone asks you to set goals, the process really is useless. Simply naming your goals doesn't provide you with any urgency regarding taking the vital next steps toward achieving them. When you eventually pull out your list to review it sometime in the future, you'll see that you didn't end up doing what you said you would, and that definitely *is* frustrating.

NOT ALL GOALS ARE CREATED EQUAL

How do you know if your goals are specific enough and contain clearly actionable measures of achievement? TARGET Goals are unambiguous goals written in a specific format, developed by my colleague David Russell and outlined in his book, *Success With People*.[1] They are precise and establish accountability to propel you forward. I use them to lay out my own road map because the process is straight-forward and covers all the important points—and it works. The structure of TARGET Goals narrows your objective into clearly defined actions and brings a sense of urgency to your daily activities, forcing you to focus on what is absolutely vital to succeed. They provide a pathway that naturally carries you from admirable ideas to productive strategies and then to realistic, measurable actions with deadlines. Following is a template for writing your own TARGET business-oriented goals.

My TARGET Business Goal

To begin: _____

Action verb: _____

Realistic

Goal: _____

Effective
measurement: _____

Time period: _____

You may want to log in to www.DPAresources.com to download your own blank TARGET Goal template so you can practice this method as you read.

Start with the word "**T**o" and follow it with an "**A**ction verb." Next, add a "**R**ealistic **G**oal" area or focus. Then add an "**E**ffective measure of success." Finally, close it with the "**T**ime period for the goal to be achieved."

Here's an example: To increase the number of clients with investable assets of $1 million or more by 10 percent before the end of the third quarter.

To begin:	*To*
Action verb:	*increase*
Realistic **G**oal:	*# of clients with investable assets of $1MM+*
Effective measurement:	*by 10 percent (eight new clients)*
Time period:	*before September 30 (end of the third quarter)*

TARGET Goals distill your objectives to:

- *what* you will do (notice the verb is always positive),

- *how* you will measure your success, and

- *when* you will complete your goal.

Although I've used a percentage for the effective measure in this example, you should use the actual number you're targeting (in this example, "eight new clients"). The more specific you can be, the better.

One of the most powerful elements of TARGET Goals is the last step: the deadline. It is key to giving your activities traction and will show you how serious you really are about reaching your desired objective.

If you announce to others that you plan to accomplish something significant, one of the first questions is always, When? When will you run your marathon? When will you graduate? When will you get married? When will you take your big trip? When will you double your current AUM? A date is real and specific, and it gives you assurance that there is a plan for this event to actually happen. Treating a date as a deadline brings more urgency, providing a day of reckoning. A deadline forces you to review your activities and be accountable for your time, with no excuses.

Deadlines make some people feel uncomfortable, and they prefer to gloss over this step or treat the time element of their TARGET Goals as a mere suggestion. They may say, "That's too specific" or, "So many things could happen that would be beyond my control, causing me to fall short" or, "Why don't we just get some of the larger activities under way, see how long they take, and then frame a realistic overall time frame from there?"

World-class athletes have an advantage that advisors can employ— the use of deadlines as motivating tools. When elite athletes are facing an important competition, they have a specific date by which they know they must be ready to perform at their peak. They develop a very narrow focus and get very specific about goal times, daily diet details, rest schedules, and training routines—all to ensure they are ready for race day. They concentrate on the particular (and demanding) activities that are relevant to what they want to achieve and repeat them on a daily basis. They keep all their efforts focused on that deadline because they know their performance day will not be postponed. They maintain absolute focus on what they are doing and why, because they know when the day comes they will be tested. If they didn't pay attention to the deadline, they simply would not perform as excellently as they do.

When I was preparing for the Olympics, I knew my race day was September 22. That deadline dictated the timing of all my efforts. My coach and I mapped the details of the work that needed to be done with a set number of weeks for fitness conditioning, strength building, and rest. The most intense time of my buildup was a grueling 14 weeks where I would push my body to its physical limit each day and then train myself to mentally keep going beyond my limit. Even though I was tired, I could commit to do the exceptionally demanding regime it took to reach my goal time because the deadline meant an end was in sight. On race day, I swam the fastest time of my life.

The work your business will demand isn't likely to be as physically or mentally demanding as an Olympic buildup, but it will take determined focus and commitment, even when you're tired or just don't feel like it. The deadline you established when you set your TARGET Goal can keep you going with just a bit more focus for a bit longer, and that will make a tremendous difference to your long-term results.

Two advisors from a large bank I worked with were expected to receive referrals from other divisions of the bank. Their manager provided them with an annual goal. We set goals for how many referrals they would seek from various bank channels by the last day of each month. When they had a narrow time frame to focus on finding their set number of referrals, they were more motivated to cultivate relationships within other divisions. They would specifically tell their colleagues the type of prospects they were looking for and ask for introductions. After several months, they found they received many more referrals than their associates who had not set deadlines for themselves. Eventually, they ended up surpassing their manager's annual target for them because they ensured they met their numbers by each monthly deadline.

Things beyond your control may very well arise, but time is going to march forward anyway, so why not draw a definite line in the sand? When you categorically identify all the elements of your TARGET Goal, you know exactly where you're going, can itemize the details of what it's going to take to get there, and know when you've achieved success. A deadline allows you to work backwards, setting relevant waypoints to track your progress, creating a timeline for your actions. The most necessary activities required to achieve your success become clearer. You have focus and a sense of urgency that make persevering through challenges more tolerable. Establishing a realistic timeline is a huge, positive step toward reaching your goals.

Perhaps you have a big goal that won't be accomplished for some time to come. TARGET Goals still work. When I was nine years old and first decided I wanted to win an Olympic medal, I needed to do a lot of growing, learning, training, and competing before I could achieve what I wanted. Even after I competed in the Los Angeles Olympics in 1984, there were still four years of hard work to be done before I would finally be ready to win a medal. I didn't realize it at the time, but starting in 1984 I used the TARGET Goal method to break down my overarching goal into individual steps. Each year I set a specific time I wanted to achieve within the next 12 months, and then broke that down further into monthly target times and training activities to condition my body to perform faster.

1988 Olympic TARGET Goal

To begin: To

Action verb: swim

Realistic
Goal: 200 meters backstroke

Effective
measurement: in 2 minutes flat

Time period: on September 22, 1988

December 1987 TARGET Goal

To begin:	*To*
Action verb:	*swim*
Realistic Goal:	*200 meters backstroke*
Effective measurement:	*in 2 minutes 2 seconds*
Time period:	*by December 31, 1987*

As I progressed, I maintained the flexibility to make changes if they were necessary, yet still easily related my short-term aims and activities to the overarching four-year goal.

When working with longer-term goals, use one TARGET Goal sheet to outline your overarching objective and then several more sheets to set checkpoints along the way to keep moving you closer to your ultimate destination. If you want to lose 30 pounds in the next six months, you might set specific monthly or even weekly goals related to your diet, the type and frequency of exercise you will do, and hours of quality sleep you will get to realistically, safely, and sustainably move you toward your 30-pound goal.

What would this look like applied to your business? Rick and I started working together when he was a brand-new independent advisor. He wanted to manage $40 million and charge an average management fee of 1 percent on a payout grid of 85 percent in order to gross $340,000.

As I encouraged you to do in the previous chapter, Rick had considered why he wanted to build his business to this size—specifically he planned to:

- Take one week off every quarter to be able to participate in running races in his region of the country.

- Take an additional three-week vacation with his family each year.

- Allocate 15 percent of his gross earnings to two charitable causes he cared deeply about. His TARGET Goal was: "To build my assets under management to $40 million by four years from today."

By having a definite date by which to achieve his goal (four years in the future), Rick got precise and gave himself a tool to gauge his progress.

KEEP BREAKING DOWN YOUR TARGET GOALS

Let's map Rick's sample TARGET Goal together.

Rick's TARGET Business Goal

To begin: *To*

Action verb: *build*

Realistic
Goal: *my assets under management*

Effective
measurement: *to $40 million*

Time period: *by four years from today*

If this were *your* goal, your next step would be to break down the four-year goal into four annual TARGET Goals. If you want to grow your business by $40 million over four years, you'll need to be adding approximately \$10 million in new assets each year. Break that down further, and you're hunting for approximately \$835,000 each month.

My TARGET Business Goal

To begin: *To*

Action verb: *acquire*

Realistic
Goal: *new client assets*

Effective
measurement: *of \$835,000*

Time period: *by the end of this month*

Now you have a monthly goal that reflects your annual target to get you to your \$40 million AUM. The \$40 million is no longer a "nice to reach someday" wishful-thinking number. You have a specific, objective, truthful way to measure your progress.

Even when you break it down to a monthly goal, you may still feel overwhelmed by the figures. Now is the time to evaluate how serious you are about your four-year TARGET Goal. The big numbers sound nice to talk about, but this is where we get real about making those big goals happen. You don't need to be frightened by what stares back at you on your TARGET Goal sheet; instead, consider it a great time to recognize that big goals require focused work and enjoy imagining what achieving them will feel like. Recognize there is no shortcut and get ready to start your journey.

When I was swimming, it would have been far easier for me to say that I wanted to make an Olympic final rather than win a medal. But I know for certain that if I had made my goal to place among the top 16 swimmers, I would never have come close to the goal time that allowed me to win my medal. My focus on my specific goal pushed me to perform at a much higher level than I would have ever done with a less definitive goal of just being among the best in the world.

Of course, even though I set a challenging goal and deeply wanted to win a medal, there was nothing I could do about any of the other competitors: I could not control how fast they were going to swim or other details about whom I would face on the day of my event. Therefore, I had to aim for something that I *could* control, and that was my goal time of two minutes. I could not get caught up thinking about how others might swim the race, how fast some had been swimming leading up to the Olympics, or even what time might qualify for the final. I just had to be clear about *my* goal time and focus all my thinking and effort on that.

As an advisor, there are many things outside of your control: markets can go up or down, other producers in your office may earn more or less than you, and so on. Whatever your circumstances, the only things you can control are *your* actions and responses. TARGET Goals help keep you focused on your aims, so you won't get distracted and spend your time and energy being concerned about other people and circumstances beyond your control.

From years of working with advisors, I know, even at this point, many still resist specifying a deadline because the fear of falling short of a formal target runs deep. Perhaps you still have nagging doubts about getting so specific about numbers, measurements, and timelines, quietly wondering, "But what if I get specific and then don't make it?"

Don't worry. If you miss your target, you miss. The world won't end, and your dog will still love you. I'm not advocating having your TARGET

Goals tattooed somewhere on your body. But if you do miss, you do want to review what you might do differently so you can improve your results in the future. Unlike competing in the Olympics, you don't have to wait four years to try to hit your goal again. (The next time you're feeling some pressure when approaching a prospect meeting consider this and use it to help you maintain perspective.)

Getting specific is worth it. And even when some advisors I know have missed their exact goal, they've come so close and created so much momentum that within a few more months they've gone on to achieve it. Although it took slightly longer than they had originally anticipated, they've told me that they never would have achieved anywhere near their goal unless they had written down exactly what they wanted to achieve and by when. They drew a line in the sand and then crossed it, achieving their goal far sooner than they would have if they hadn't committed.

What you do on a daily basis adds up, making a big difference in the long term. Some months you may end up ahead of your target and other months behind it, but by tracking with specific numbers you'll know exactly how you're progressing. You'll more easily spot the little distractions that are easy to gloss over or justify when you don't track your daily activities closely to your TARGET Goal. Instead of waiting until you are far from where you need to be along your path before taking any corrective action, you can easily make tweaks to your daily activities because you will see how they are directly impacting your annual goal and, ultimately, your overarching long-term TARGET Goal. Turn your doubt about making your goal on its head by asking yourself, What if I DO make it?

STRETCH BUT DON'T SNAP

In the process of your planning and dreaming, make sure you do a reality check. Some advisors want to build huge businesses but aren't realistic about the time it's going to take. Perhaps they like the sound of big numbers but don't have a realistic picture of the process involved to actually achieve them, or don't understand that achieving them would require a dramatic change in how they operate their business. Sometimes they're afraid that if they don't name an exceptionally large objective, their manager will think they're not motivated enough. This unconsidered approach only leads to disappointment. On the other hand, some advisors have the ability to reach bold goals but are lazy and don't want to do the work those goals will require. They set goals that are way too easy and never stretch out of their comfort zone to realize their potential.

Your TARGET Goals need to be realistic, and you need to be honest about how much work you're able and willing to do. While I'm encouraging you to dream, I want you to *reach* your dreams. Your goals must be measurable *and* reasonable. They should stretch you and make you a little nervous when considering the pursuit, yet be real enough that you can clearly envision the exhilaration of achieving them.

Goals should be closer to *possible*, but not too far from *probable*. If they're closer to probable, they might be too easy for you to achieve.

MAKING IT YOURS

Building your business definitely takes focus, energy, and concentration, but it is worth it. A lot of people spend too much time thinking about what they want, what they'll do, and how they are going to do it, yet fail to actually start taking concrete action.

Begin today by moving forward to what it is *you* wish to achieve. Create or download (from www.DPAresources.com) a blank TARGET Goal template and begin determining what your business needs to look like to allow you the success you pictured for yourself in Chapter 1. What needs to happen in the next four years? After imagining clearly how that will feel, name what needs to be accomplished one year from now for you to track toward that success and break that down on another TARGET Goal template. Then to achieve that one-year picture, what has to happen within the next 30 days? Write down some thoughts. These notes are for you; no one else needs to see them. Just make some quiet time for yourself and write them down. Don't rush this; consider them for a couple of days, refining your drafts to specify practical actions that will get you to your vision of success.

Review your TARGET Goals regularly so you can identify distractions more clearly. I keep my TARGET Goals on my phone, so I can easily scroll through them at the beginning of each day to keep me focused on where I'm headed.

DISTRACTION-PROOF STEPS

1. Use TARGET Goals.

2. Make time to record what you want and by when.

3. Keep your goals where you can see them every day.

Athletes have the advantage of knowing exactly when performance day is coming. They have it firmly planted in their mind and use it to keep motivated and accountable when distractions, new ideas, and negative thoughts vie for their attention. You can use the TARGET Goal method to be just as specific about your objectives and deadlines in both your business and personal life, giving you the same advantage in reaching your picture of success.

After you've set your TARGET Goals, you're ready to move to the next step in building your business: getting specific about what's going to bring in the relationships you want and the money you need.

CHAPTER THREE
CHOOSE YOUR PATH

*"You will never reach your destination if you stop
and throw stones at every dog that barks."*

– WINSTON CHURCHILL, BRITISH STATESMAN AND PRIME MINISTER
OF THE UNITED KINGDOM, 1940–1945 AND 1951–1955

By offering too many investment options for clients, you'll be distracted
by:

- Researching investment choices outside your area of expertise to answer prospects' and clients' questions

- Monitoring too many investment choices, leaving little or no time for hunting new business

- Lack of focus, which will dilute your conviction for your process

The most successful advisors never try to be all things to all people. They
consciously determine their specialty, develop key relationships with
complementary professional service providers, and focus on prospects

who are good fits for their business. They would much rather let inappropriate prospects walk away than spend their own time and energy on activities outside their areas of concentration. They choose their path to success and get where they are going by persevering along that track. This chapter will help you determine how you want to structure your business and develop conviction for your area of focus.

Advisors face a constant flow of new ideas regarding prospecting, relationship building, ideal clients, pricing, staffing, compliance, cross-selling, on-selling, onboarding, fee-based versus transaction-based models, indexing, market timing, alpha, beta, fixed income, interest rates, equities, muni bonds, and corporate bonds. In your spare time, you can review UITs, REITs, ETFs, and MLPs and assess whether any of this alphabet soup could work in your business. Are you feeling dizzy yet?

The overwhelming choices regarding how you can structure your business, what products you can offer, and which systems you can use to service your clients can make your head spin. Many of the choices are excellent, but you can quickly get caught up in researching and testing new options, thinking you're making progress in your business, when in fact you're only being distracted from moving closer to your objective with your current processes, services, and activities. A good analogy might be a visit to your local grocery store, in which you randomly put things in your cart as you walk down the aisles and think you've had a successful and efficient shopping outing. Yes, your cart will be full and you'll pay for what you have selected, but you likely will have things you will never use and not vital staples you really need—and you will have wasted your money and time. A better option is to cut through the clutter of the myriad things you *could* do and focus on those that are *best* for you to do because they are most conducive to what you want to do.

As we discussed in the last chapter, serious athletes have the advantage of a deadline. While many different combinations of approaches and exercises might work, athletes don't have the time to keep jumping from one training method to the next, forever experimenting with new techniques. Because they face a date on which they must perform, they seek counsel from coaches and others who have achieved at the level they are aiming for, then thoughtfully choose the specific activities they believe will best prepare them for what they want to achieve, and finally commit to consistently practicing those activities. They don't have any guarantees that their choices will be the *perfect* ones, but because the clock is ticking they focus on what seems sensible, logical, and best suited to their objectives. Then, they work diligently, becoming more proficient each day. They see improvements, and this increases their confidence in their ability to achieve their objectives, which further motivates them to commit to their selected courses. They might tweak the details here or there, but they do not deviate from their chosen core activities and processes.

Because you crafted your objective as a TARGET Goal, you have a deadline too. Hold yourself accountable; treat your deadline as seriously as an athlete does. Recognize that you do not have time to be continually experimenting with investment rationales, service offerings, or client management systems. Seek advice from successful advisors and industry experts and then pick your path. There will be other business models and methods you could have picked, but if you do diligent research and select what feels like a good and prudent fit to get you where you want to go, then commit to it. Make choices you feel confident will allow you to be a financial advisor who enjoys running your business—instead of letting it run you ragged—and who has time to spend helping clients pursue and enjoy financial peace of mind.

BE DECISIVE ABOUT YOUR CHOICES

When speaking and coaching, I highlight the need for successful advisors to be both wonderfully relational and ruthlessly clinical. You are running a business, and while good relationships are vital to your success, the ability to make objective, fiscally wise choices is equally important. When selecting what services to include in your mix of offerings, it's time to be decisive. Make your choices and stick to them. There are too many options to think you can offer every type of financial product or platform that people may want and effectively pay attention to them all. In addition to copious investment choices from which to select, you will need to decide what other services you want to offer, such as financial planning, estate planning, cash management, college funding planning, or client budgeting services. Then there's also a range of insurances to consider, from life to long-term care to disability, just to name a select few. Mortgages, business lending, and loan refinancing offer even more options. This is far from an exhaustive list of products and services to choose from to build your path.

When I started as a financial advisor, my partner had already been in the industry five years and knew she wanted to continue building the business around financial planning. We both enjoyed developing deep relationships with our clients and their families. We had good financial planning software that allowed us to provide in-depth analysis of their current situations and effective guidance in planning for the future. This approach helped us gain a holistic understanding of their financial situations and gradually led to our managing the complete financial assets of most of our clients. Because our focus was on providing advice related to larger life issues, we knew that watching daily stock fluctuations and tracking short-term market performance were distractions for us.

Instead, we chose to use carefully selected third-party money managers, as well as a couple of exchange-traded fund (ETF) and mutual fund models. While we could speak cogently regarding insurance, we relied on trusted outside vendors to cover this area of our business. There were wholesalers who eagerly showed us how we could generate attractive income using their products, and while they had some good ideas, their offerings were not what we had chosen to focus on in our business. There were colleagues in our office who had very different models they had chosen to build their businesses, and while their methods worked for them, we had selected our course. We did what we enjoyed, felt like we offered true value to our clients, and were profitable. We didn't need or want to keep tweaking our business model.

Some advisors object to limiting their business models to a narrow range of choices because they think it will cost them business. They worry that unless they accommodate a broad variety of people and range of desires they won't be able to get the number of clients they need to sustain their business. This is a fallacy—don't buy into it! As I mentioned at the start of this chapter, you don't need to be all things to all people, because not all people are your ideal clients. (We'll talk specifically about how to identify ideal clients in the next chapter.) There will be some people who want things you don't offer and that's okay; they can find someone else who will meet their needs.

If you know your process works, there will be plenty of people who will be attracted to your focus and conviction. If you are specific about your approach and can clearly articulate your rationale, it will help, not hinder, your business. People are looking for advisors—they want you to offer your advice and recommend an investment approach you are confident is suitable for them. There are enough people who need and want your help the way you choose to provide it.

Don't think you have to develop a new or unique money management mix when you choose how to shape your business. Whether you're in a large wire house or you're an independent advisor, find colleagues you respect and ask what offerings they focus on and how they work. With LinkedIn and the social chatter you likely have access to from your broker-dealer or parent company, finding people who have done what you want to do isn't difficult. Seek them out, post questions in appropriate groups, make time to talk with people on brief phone calls, and talk to colleagues at conferences. Find out what money management styles have been successful for them. Then, select the main products and platforms that you believe will enable you to build and sustain the business you want and focus on those.

Recently, after I spoke at an event for advisors from a large U.S. bank, I stayed to listen to a panel discussion with a number of successful, seasoned advisors, each with several decades of experience. They were all working on the retail advisory side of the business at the time, but several of them had moved back and forth between the retail and wholesale sides of the industry over the years. All of them had depth as well as length of practice in financial services. When asked, "Knowing what you know now, what would you do differently if you had to build your business all over again?" every panelist agreed they would narrow the investment options they offered to clients, choosing a core platform of model portfolios from the beginning and allocating all of their clients' assets into those options. They said there just was no need to offer more and that doing so had made operating their businesses unnecessarily difficult.

REMEMBER WHY YOU'RE DOING WHAT YOU'RE DOING

Remember your vision of the kind of life you want to live and the resources you want your business to generate. Plan to offer products, platforms, and services that enable you to provide helpful advice and investment guidance to your clients as well as enjoy the lifestyle you want. All advisors I know who offer complex or broad ranges of investment processes feel frazzled and overwhelmed to a degree that just isn't necessary. You want an offering that is flexible, yet manageable enough to allow you time to focus on getting your optimal number of ideal clients. If you are a one- to three-person advisory business, developing a scalable process is vital so that you can continue to deliver consistently high-quality service as your number of clients grows *and* have a workload that remains sustainable and enjoyable.

VISUALIZE WHAT YOUR BUSINESS MIGHT LOOK LIKE

Perhaps you have access to third-party money managers and just want to use several of them. Or, maybe you subscribe to modern portfolio theory and decide to stick to a basic asset allocation process that focuses on an appropriate balance of stocks, bonds, and cash relative to clients' risk tolerances. Develop a selection of five or six portfolios that are straightforward and effective and allow you to meet the needs of a variety of clients. You can walk clients through a thorough risk profile questionnaire to determine which portfolio would suit them best. At one end of your spectrum, you might offer a total fixed-income portfolio for those who are retired and value principal preservation over significant returns. At the other end, you might offer a portfolio that is completely allocated to equities. Beware of building such a portfolio with individual equities that will require you to spend too much time monitoring many positions. It can be more desirable to index and use a cluster of ETFs or low-cost mutual funds and let the dedicated money managers who watch equities 24/7 do the monitoring for you. That way you can spend the majority of your time focused on providing more comprehensive advice and finding more ideal clients rather than stock trading. Whatever you choose to offer, know your rationale and where elements fit into your overall picture. Ensure you can explain these things so your clients clearly understand what you are recommending and why it makes sense for them.

Often, advisors can be so focused on securing new assets, they don't clarify at an initial exploratory meeting that they offer a range of model portfolios and expect clients to adhere to that investment process and allow reallocation of any existing assets as necessary to do this. Then, once they have the new assets under management there are often lots of excuses why they don't insist on reallocation, or they simply don't get around to doing it. While these advisors may say the idea of having model portfolios is appealing, they do not make placing clients in them a priority at the beginning of the relationship and before long have an unwieldy hodge-podge of dozens of stocks, mutual funds, ETFs, and other investments covering various asset classes. Remember, you have a fiduciary responsibility to your clients: you are on the hook for watching performance and providing feedback about any assets your clients have entrusted to you. If you get caught up in needing to scrutinize hundreds of individual investments, you won't have the time you need to actively build your business, nor the capacity to effectively service new clients, even if they happen to come in without any direct effort from you. You'll be exhausted, stressed, and frustrated—not good for you or your clients!

Find people who are interested in what you are offering and willing to follow your advice. From the beginning of your relationship, before any forms are signed, explain your process and why you adhere to the method and systems you have chosen to use. If you've decided to take a holistic approach to your advising, clarify that following your process allows you time to tend to your clients' big-picture financial needs and most important life issues. If prospects are not open to having their money managed your way, they are not ideal clients for you—let them go.

On very, very rare occasions, you may decide to provide a client investment choices outside your core stable of portfolios. Always make this decision cautiously and with good reason. Perhaps you believe it is worth your extra time and energy to provide a very select few large clients with the opportunity to invest in individual equities. Maybe you have a client who is a retired executive from a significant, industry-leading company. They have a large amount of assets with you and appreciate and follow your advice. However, they also have a feel for their particular industry, track current business activities, and see good possibilities for future earnings of a company in the industry and want to own shares. Or, maybe a high-value prospect holds sizeable low-cost-basis stock positions in solid companies. Make sure these people understand that you normally do not accommodate investments outside your portfolios, but you are prepared to do it for them, as long as they follow your recommendations when the appropriate time to sell comes. They must recognize you are not going to be watching a screen all day to see any price changes. Perhaps you have some really great clients who want to put money into alternative investments. In that case, you may want to consider offering a couple of managed futures funds, hedge funds, or real estate portfolios run by specialists in those areas.

The next chapter will address identifying your ideal client in detail, but your ideal client should always fit into your models. If you do make exceptions to your models, ensure they are indeed exceptions and don't gradually become normative. Have a considered, strategic reason for broadening the path you previously selected and committed to follow.

SHOULD YOU OFFER FINANCIAL PLANNING?

Another area to consider is whether or not you will offer financial planning. Some advisors won't take a prospect as a client until they first do a formal financial plan. While most clients assume advisors will give them at least some level of financial guidance, not all clients want a formal, detailed financial plan. Decide how much you want to emphasize this service. If you want to take a holistic approach, advising clients on important life issues such as college education or retirement funding, cash flow, and social security, you likely want to develop a deeper planning process. You will need to determine how you will shape your discovery and planning system, including the software you will use. This is another great time to ask others what they use and like: talk with advisors within your company who specialize in financial planning and see what they are doing or ask questions on social media groups. Whether you use a proprietary platform provided by your firm or one of the commercially available programs, get comfortable with the system so you can use it effectively.

Preparing financial plans can uncover assets you may not otherwise know about. It demonstrates that you don't watch market movements all day, but instead focus on your clients' broader, long-term financial pictures. Your comprehensive understanding of clients' current financial situations and future hopes, and your competent advising across these areas, moves you way beyond a stock trader or a robo-advisor and makes you a trusted advisor to your clients, a true partner in their financial lives. Realize that other advisors are going to court your clients and that you likely will have a few clients who used to work with someone else. Financial planning is a great way to deepen your relationships with your clients, helping minimize the possibility that they may switch to another advisor because they know and intimately trust you.

I am a strong proponent for financial planning because it allows advisors to gain a very clear picture of their clients' financial circumstances, especially when they review clients' personal balance sheets and cash flow. Often a client doesn't realize their own complete financial situation, and planning can be enlightening for them as well as for their advisor. Also, I have personally experienced the business advantages of planning. And as I mentioned earlier, many advisors have built successful businesses taking other tracks. Regardless of your preference, make business choices that suit what you want to offer clients and know why you operate your business the way you do.

EXPAND YOUR EXPERTISE

Get a feel for how four or five analysts see the world, then gather resources from the core voices you respect. Read their monthly updates, so you get a complete picture about what is happening socially and economically, both nationally and globally. Develop a method to gain a broad overview without getting overwhelmed by what can be interesting but time-consuming details. At review meetings arrive well equipped to share up-to-date information and useful commentary to help clients gain a better perspective and deeper understanding of current market activities and future outlooks. By consistently referring to the same carefully selected group of analysts, you'll save time when you want to get reliable, trustworthy updates because you can quickly turn to your go-to group, whose sites you will have bookmarked on your computer.

DEVELOP YOUR ALLIANCES

You've decided how you are going to shape your business and manage your time, with a clear rationale behind what investment platforms and advisory services you choose to offer. Even if you aim to take a comprehensive approach to your advising, clients will need more services than you personally can offer. In addition to making investments for clients, trusted advisors are also aggregators of information and a source of referrals to other trustworthy service providers. If clients have any need in their financial lives, whether you handle that area or not, you want them coming to you for advice first. This is when you need a team, your own network of like-minded specialists to whom you feel comfortable referring your clients. Not only is this great for your clients and helps deepen their view of you as their go-to advisor, this referral network should also provide you a channel of qualified prospects to grow your business.

Some of your clients may need a Certified Public Accountant (CPA) or an estate attorney. If you don't provide insurance help to clients, they may need to know good agents who offer life, disability, long-term care, or any other type of insurance you believe would be important for them to consider. Maybe your clients have business banking or mortgage needs. Get to know some of these specialists in your neighborhood or even in your own firm if you work at a large organization. Start a relationship focused on the high-quality referrals you can *give*, rather than asking if they have clients to send your way.

Call or email a few people, introducing yourself and letting them know that your business is growing. Say you're looking to get to know other professionals who specialize in services that you don't offer but that your clients need. Explain you want to build a small but effective network of other professionals you know and to whom you feel comfortable and confident referring your clients. Inquire if they're currently working with an advisor who does what you do. Ask them if they would be interested in talking further to explore possible opportunities to share referrals. If so, tell them you would appreciate taking them out for coffee and learning more about them and what they offer their clients.

At the meeting, be the one asking the questions so you can sense whether or not this could be a good, profitable fit for both of you. You want to interview them to see if they would be a good member of your team. Clarify that you want to assemble a number of specialists who share your approach to clients and would like to build a mutually beneficial relationship. Let them know you are looking for a set number of ideal clients and describe that type of person to them. Find out about their ideal clients and the typical business issues those clients face. Determine where they usually find new clients. Be specific and listen for signs that they understand you and know how to help you in the way you wish to receive help.

As you assemble your referral team, look for opportunities to both give and receive value from the relationships. Show them you're serious and deliberate about reaching your own goals *and* you are committed to helping them. Introduce the members to each other to assist them in benefiting from cross-referrals. Ask them if they do complimentary assessments or reviews of existing clients' insurance policies or loans, and

PROFESSIONALS IN YOUR NETWORK

Developing alliances with other professionals is a great way to expand the areas where you can help your clients with expert advice. Some types of professionals you might want to consider exploring relationships with include:

- CPAs

- Estate attorneys

- Divorce attorneys

- Insurance brokers

- Mortgage brokers

- Funeral home directors

- College planners

- Elder care attorneys

see how flexible and accommodating they are. As you come across articles that can help your team members stay abreast of changes in the financial industry—perhaps about issues such as business owner tax changes, updated retirement plan funding thresholds, or new developments regarding education loans—send them a copy with an attached note saying something like, "Saw this yesterday and have been telling some of my clients about it. Thought it might be of interest to you and some of your clients." If you provide your clients with a quarterly economic review, send your team members a copy to keep them abreast of your perspective. These types of helpful communications will give them a greater taste for how you help your clients and make it easier for them to refer their clients to you.

DISTRACTION-PROOF STEPS

1. Maintain a specific, carefully chosen investment platform and service offering.

2. Choose clients who will fit your model and work with you the way you want to work.

3. Build an effective, professional referral group.

Create your investment system and stick to it. Have a set rationale and know your structure so you are not tempted to constantly tweak it to accommodate prospects who just aren't appropriate for you. Once you have decided on your specific platform and products, develop your expertise and relationships to become your clients' go-to expert for all financial matters. You don't have to do everything yourself, but you can provide your clients with a full spectrum of services they need by providing referrals to your network of other trustworthy professionals.

Keep your focus on the path you have chosen so you can make positive progress toward your vision and meet your goal by your deadline. Next, we'll look at how to find the right number of the ideal people to join you on that path.

CHAPTER FOUR
SHARPEN YOUR FOCUS

"The successful warrior is the average man, with laser-like focus."
– BRUCE LEE, MARTIAL ARTIST, ACTOR, AND FILMMAKER

Without a clear picture of your ideal client, you'll succumb to distractions such as:

- Providing small or unprofitable clients your best (and most time-consuming) level of service

- Spending precious time considering (or worse, onboarding) referrals who aren't a good fit for your business

- Using valuable mental energy wondering if you're serving your best clients appropriately (and worrying that you're not)

- Any new idea because you think it could suit a *couple* of your clients

You're off to a fantastic start with a clear vision for what you want to achieve and a path of investment choices and services to realize that vision sooner.

You've recognized the need for a scalable system so you can sanely manage a large number of clients, even if you don't have a large team to handle it all. Now, let's bring that focus on your chosen path into high resolution by thinking critically about who the clients joining you on your journey will be and how you will find them.

As I mentioned before, I don't have many of the typical physical characteristics of great swimmers, such as exceptionally long arms or big feet. Through my years of swimming, I trained with guys who had much more natural ability in the water than I did. They looked the part, talked about big dreams, and had great potential. But when training got challenging, they would regularly cut the prescribed number of meters to swim or reps of dry-land exercises. The quality of their work was also poor: they'd settle for putting out 50 percent effort when the coach had asked for 80 percent. They regularly took shortcuts and justified it to themselves with excuses like, "I'm tired, and I wasn't even going to come to training today. So, this is better than having done nothing." The necessary numbers and quality related to the work assigned by the coach were clear; they just chose to regularly ignore these. Then when international teams were chosen, they never made the cut. Because they took shortcuts, made excuses rather than doing the work, and continually told themselves, "Close enough is good enough," they never realized their full potential. In this chapter we'll look at how to identify the numbers you require and ascertain prospects' quality so you can get the clients you want and, as a result, the money you need to ensure you realize your big dreams.

KNOW YOUR NUMBERS

Now that you've settled on your initial mix of services and financial product offerings, it's time to get down to the numbers. Ultimately, your business is a numbers game: you need to have a minimum number of clients with a certain level of assets to achieve your goals and to generate the income necessary to keep your door open and food on your table. Know your numbers. When they are specific, clear, and prominent in your thoughts, they will sharpen your focus, fuel your drive, and strengthen your conviction to implement your strategy to find those people as soon as possible. Knowing your numbers might sound obvious, but that's why I emphasize it—we often rush past what is obvious and don't give it the attention it needs.

Much has been written in our industry highlighting the importance of relationships and trust. It is certainly true that as you develop rapport with your clients, they will come to trust you more deeply with greater assets and be more likely to refer you to others. As we touched on in the last chapter, being relational is a crucial part of what advisors must do if they want to be successful. However, it is only a part. As you are growing your business, you might develop wonderful relationships with clients, but you're going to struggle if you don't have the right *number* of great relationships. If you have two or three deep relationships with people who really love working with you, that feels good, but unless they entrust you with a significant level of assets, you're not going to make it. When you are just getting started as an advisor, it's highly unlikely successful business people with large assets are going to give you everything they have to manage. We'll talk more in the next chapter about how to confidently approach prospects, even when you don't have years of experience under your belt. For now let's get your mindset fine-tuned and back to needing to be ruthless, in this case regarding the precise number of clients you are hunting to meet your goals within your specified time.

When you talk with prospects, you are always wonderfully relational, engaging them with questions and carefully listening as they respond. Track details on your mental checklist to decide if they would be clients you'd enjoy working with. Would spending time on bringing these people into your fold of clients be a good investment on your part? Because your time is limited, consider this question unemotionally: be ruthlessly analytical as you honestly and judiciously determine how to allocate your time in pursuit of your ideal clients.

THE TRIPLE-A APPROACH

When I first began advising at Morgan Stanley, we focused much of our energy on developing what the company called Triple-A clients because they had what was called an Active Assets Account. As time went on and account names changed, my partner and I continued to use the Triple-A client classification as a way to identify our ideal clients, borrowing from Duncan MacPherson and David Miller's Pareto System classifications, detailed in their book *Breakthrough Business Development*.[1] Triple-A clients:

- have your desired level of *assets*,

- have the right *attitude*, and

- will become *advocates* for you.

This provides an excellent strategy for filtering prospects and identifying those who will help you build a great business and reach your objective sooner. Let's take a closer look at each.

Assets

Staying with the example we introduced in Chapter 2, growing your business by $40 million over four years means bringing in approximately $10 million of new assets annually. Some people might break that down to 10 clients bringing in $1 million each. While the numbers fit neatly and make it convenient to project forward, I have yet to find that happening so tidily in the real world. More realistically, you'll probably end up with clients with a range of assets. Pull out your pen and paper and start setting down some possible numbers. How many client relationships do you want to manage? What account size is in your "sweet spot"? Do you want to manage accounts of between $1.5 million and $2.5 million? Is $500K to $1 million a more realistic focus for you at this point? What are you and your business equipped to handle?

Perhaps you decide to work with clients who have accounts valued at a minimum of $250,000, going up to $1 million at the higher end. Let's say your average account size is $500,000. Doing the math, you need to add 20 new clients to your business each year with an average asset level of $500,000. But let's drill down another layer and get more specific about what that might look like. Your numbers could be different; multiple combinations will work. These are simply presented as an example to get you thinking about your goals and to show the importance of being specific:

- Two clients with $1 million+ each of assets to manage ($2MM+)

- Five clients with $800,000 to $1 million of assets to manage ($4MM+)

- Eight clients with $500,000 to $800,000 of assets to manage ($4MM+)

- Total of 15 new clients with $10 million+ of assets to manage

Come up with numbers that feel like a good fit for you, with asset levels and numbers of clients that seem reachable. Remember that you are looking to build your business. While you may accept clients with $250,000 in assets, those are not the size of accounts you are actively seeking. Keep focused on your sweet spot regarding asset levels to develop a manageable core of clients. This will help ensure you don't overload your book with a large number of minimally profitable clients.

Select your final numbers and *write down* the details. Don't just hold them in your head—actually write them down. Most advisors won't bother to do this, but something powerful happens when you make a strong enough commitment to put your numbers in writing, so go ahead and take this step to give yourself an advantage. Seeing actual account values recorded and specific numbers of real-life clients makes your longer-term objective quantifiable and clear. Now you're not after some vague value of assets and an obscure, unknown number of people to grow your business: you have a measureable target. You're hunting for 15 clients who have specific assets. You can still develop wonderful relationships, but now you know *who* your clients need to be and exactly *how many* you need to keep you on track.

You know over the next 12 months you only need to find the *right* 15 people. Simple? Yes. Easy? Maybe, or maybe not. But that doesn't really matter. The important question is, "Is it possible?" At fewer than two people per month, the answer is, "Absolutely!" After doing this for each of the next four years, you'll be closer to the business you desire. If you're willing to work diligently and stay focused, this is definitely feasible. If you prefer to make excuses, blame markets, and get timid, you're going to struggle. Finding the right 15 people each year will take application, but the results will be worth it. Imagine how you will feel when you locate and begin helping those fortunate 15: you'll have the business you want and can enjoy those benefits you dreamed about when you got started. You'll also have potentially transformative influence on your clients' lives—impact that may shape the destinies of generations to come.

By relying on this framework, you're not going to fool yourself when you're talking with prospects who have asset levels between $100,000 and $200,000. You may like them and decide to develop a friendship or two, but you know these people will not be a part of the mix you need to achieve for your target of 15 new clients. Keep your client criteria definitively established in your heart and mind. With your quantifiable number of ideal clients and account size defined, you can use the Triple-A approach to further refine what the people joining you on your path will look like.

Attitude

If you meet a prospect who has $1 million, they definitely have the right level of assets you're targeting. Your next job is to see if they have the right attitude. This is probably your most important qualifier—even more significant that asset levels.

The "right attitude" aligns with *your* attitude about how you work with your clients. Do they understand and agree with your investing philosophy? Do they appreciate your approach and want to follow your advice? Do they feel like someone you'd want to have a long-term business relationship with? Or, do they want to spend hours telling you about their brother "who is just flying with his online account" and pressure you about producing returns like his? Do they expect constant accessibility to you but just want a listening ear to complain about how much their family members irritate them? Do they want to continually pry you for your opinions and recommendations, but refuse to make changes in their investments to match your model portfolios?

You only want 15 people to join you this year, with each one taking a reserved, exclusive spot. Don't give their places away to just anyone. Over and over I've heard advisors say they didn't have a great feeling about someone from the start, but they really wanted their assets and so took them on. They're never happy they did it. Inevitably these clients become a burden you wish you didn't have to deal with: you avoid calling them to set up meetings and even thinking about it makes you queasy. Your heart sinks when you see their name on caller ID. Don't let people who don't have the right attitude waste your time, energy, and emotion. Quite simply, those "prospects" aren't prospects. They don't make the cut and don't get to become your client, even if they have the right level of assets. Politely close the conversation and be happy that you are one meeting closer to finding your next client.

The right combination of assets and attitude is key in deciding whether a prospect would make a good client.

- Assets – Attitude = Let them walk.

- Assets + Attitude = Sign 'em up and bring 'em on board.

- Low assets – Attitude = Don't get distracted—move on.

- Low assets + Attitude = Possible—under some special circumstances. If they don't have the assets but have a great attitude, there may occasionally be other compelling reasons to take them on (more about this in Chapter 7).

Advocacy

The final "A" in the Triple-A approach to finding your ideal clients is advocacy. The most effective way to build your business is to have happy clients who become sources of referrals. The best time to clarify this expectation is from the beginning of your relationship. At your initial meeting with your prospects when you are explaining your business approach, including your client criteria and investment rationale, be direct and tell them what you want. Following is a sample conversation:

As I mentioned, the third "A" in my process is to have my clients become advocates for how I help them. [Don't say "what I do" here—you want them to understand that you build partnership relationships with your clients, not provide them with a simple commodity.] Certainly, that ball is in my court. Most of my new clients come to me by referrals and are friends or family of existing clients.

It's appropriate, not pushy, and clarifies that the person you're with is a good fit and part of an exclusive group of people who work with you. It's effective, and importantly, you won't risk alienating potential or existing clients as you would with some other suggested referral request phrases out there.

You might add, "If your tennis partner always boasts about how he's making a killing flipping stocks online, please don't mention my name to him!" This light-heartedly helps further explain who you work with by telling clients who you *won't* work with. Your new clients feel even more valued when they understand that you trust them to be discerning about recommending you.

TO NICHE OR NOT TO NICHE?

There are two distinct schools of thought about identifying prospects. Some advisors believe the service they offer is good for anybody (as long as they have the correct assets and attitude). While they are still discriminating about who they accept as clients, they don't focus on people in one particular profession and so are eager to talk to anyone to find out who might be a good fit for them. These advisors are good problem solvers, like dealing with variety, and figure that they never know where they may find their next great client. It doesn't make sense to them to limit themselves to only working with doctors or lawyers or pilots. The other approach has advisors exclusively targeting one particular market segment, such as small business owners, athletes, or surgeons. Because people in the same industry often have similar needs, concerns, or complexities (such as nuances regarding retirement benefits or stock options from a particular company), these advisors can set up duplicable systems that address their clients' common issues and be viewed as an expert in that area. Focusing on a target niche also makes it easier for clients to recommend you to others: "My advisor specializes in working with teachers; you should talk to her."

Either approach can work; choose what is comfortable for you. Regardless of whether you decide to focus on a niche or not, your Triple-A criteria should always remain your most important filter for taking on new clients. You must keep in mind the parameters for your ideal client. You now have your various products, platforms, and approach you're working with in place, and you're looking for your right 15. I lean toward taking the general approach, especially if you're just beginning in this business and want to reach your vision as soon as possible; there are simply more people across a broad spectrum of professions than there are in any single market segment. But again, either approach can work well. It comes down to how you meet people, where you find them, and the ease with which you open conversations that evolve into meaningful dialogues and result in bringing on profitable clients.

DISTRACTION-PROOF STEPS

1. Know the number of clients you're hunting.

2. Have a good reason for permitting each person to work with you.

3. Continually look for your next client.

Specifically determine what it's going to take to build the business that you want and be committed enough to it to put it in writing. Then, go earnestly searching for prospects with the right assets and attitude who you are confident will become strong advocates for you. Your time and energy are your most precious resources, and you only want a select number of new clients, so focus on people who meet your criteria. If you are talking to someone who doesn't fit, move on and know you are one person closer to your next ideal client. Don't think for one minute that people you desire to work with won't come on board with you. Keep your mental picture clear about how you will feel once you have your select group on board and stay excited about what lies ahead.

Thinking about bringing new people on board is always fun, but making those thoughts reality can be daunting. Meeting new people and comfortably engaging with them is one of the biggest concerns for advisors. Many struggle in this area. In the next chapter, we will review some specific, effective, and realistic ways to do this well.

CHAPTER FIVE

BE DELIBERATE WITH YOUR DIALOGUE

"Communication is a skill that you can learn. It's like riding a bicycle or typing. If you're willing to work at it, you can rapidly improve the quality of every part of your life."

– BRIAN TRACY, PERSONAL DEVELOPMENT SPEAKER AND AUTHOR

I f you don't commit to learning and using the best words in critical conversations with both clients and prospects, you'll be distracted by:

- Scrambling for words to articulate your value

- Talking about yourself instead of gathering valuable information about your prospects and clients

- Thinking about what you'll say next rather than truly listening

The two most important conversation skills are being genuinely interested in the person you're talking with and listening to what that person says to you. Without these foundations, you are not likely to make any meaningful connection with other people. They probably won't feel heard, and you will remember little of what they told you. Your conversation won't amount to much more than small talk. Great client relationships are built on open, frank, and personal conversations, not on small talk. Great advisors use great questions (and listen closely to the answers) to generate meaningful exchanges and develop lasting connections. So far, you've been deliberate about what you want your business to look like, what you're going to offer, and who you want as clients. Now it's time to start connecting with people to find those ideal clients. Once in a while, when you tell people that you are a financial advisor, they might light up and tell you they've been looking for someone to work with. This probably won't happen often enough to reliably get the new clients you need. A better strategy is to get in front of people and have deliberate, influential conversations with them. You want to be able to convince them to act on your advice. To be an effective advisor who provides real help, you will have to dig to find out what makes people tick. What circumstances have impacted their lives? What are their deep concerns that you can address?

"But I don't want to seem pushy."

"I don't want to put someone on the spot."

"I just don't feel comfortable talking with people I don't know."

I've heard lots of excuses for avoiding these kinds of conversations, especially with strangers. If you want to grow your business, though, you'll need to find and connect with new prospects. Being able to have effective conversations is a skill advisors must develop. Fortunately, it is something you can learn, and the more you practice, the better you will become. So, what *do* you say without doing a hard sell or sounding pushy?

Most advisors I know genuinely want to help people, and that's a great place to start. Significant conversations come much more often and naturally when you are more interested in learning about the other person than you are in impressing them with information about you or your business. Generally, people like talking about themselves: it's a topic they know a lot about, and they are confident they know the answers to questions that might be asked. So, start by asking deliberate questions. Have a plan. Know in advance what you are going to say when you have the opportunity to communicate with prospects and clients, so you can speak clearly and confidently.

Top sportspeople know what to expect on competition day. This is another practice of elite athletes that you can adopt to give you an edge in becoming an excellent advisor. Well before they turn up to compete, these athletes have practiced their performance dozens of different ways and already know how they will respond in any of the situations they might face. They have deliberate routines, planning and anticipating even seemingly little details, from pre-travel habits, to systematic methods for checking gear, to the menu for their morning meal on competition day. They are prepared. Every detail is considered and purposeful. Nothing is left to chance.

Likewise, you want to know what to expect when it's your time to "perform." When you meet a prospect, you want to have a natural conversation, but you also want to anticipate how your conversation will go. Know in advance what you will say, be sure of the most effective words to use, and confidently expect prospects' possible responses. Develop your plan for how to guide a conversation so a prospect sees your value and recognizes their need for your help. Have a practiced routine that shows you are confident with considered and purposeful questions and responses.

Being prepared doesn't mean stiffly reciting memorized lines regardless of what the other person says. It does mean you can be relaxed because you're not nervous about what happens next; you've practiced this conversation hundreds of times before, not just in your imagination but also out loud. You know what the words sound like and how it feels to say them. You can look forward to being at functions where you don't know anybody and applying your process as you meet new people. You can be a better listener because you don't have to concentrate on coming up with the next thing to say while the other person is talking. You are confident about what's coming next, so you can discipline yourself to really hear what the person is saying and wait for him or her to finish the last words of each sentence. *Then* you can meaningfully respond. If you master how to effectively communicate with people, you will thrive in much more than just your business-building activities.

Remember your goal: You're looking for 15 people to bring on board as clients—but they need to be the right 15. The more people you talk with, the more likely you are to find those perfect 15 who meet all your criteria in regards to assets, attitude, and advocacy. You're being ruthlessly analytical in finding them *and* wonderfully relational while meeting as many people as you can. It requires you to talk to many more than 18 or 20 people to find your perfect 15. But with a practiced routine, just like the athlete, you'll be completely and confidently ready when the time comes to perform. Opportunities for conversations will start happening everywhere. Thomas J. Stanley and William D. Danko's *The Millionaire Next Door* is a great book to open your eyes to why it's important to be comfortable talking to anyone. (Hint: Not all millionaires drive BMWs or wear Rolex watches; in fact, most don't.)

LEARN YOUR LINES

Recommendations for lines to use in exploratory conversations with prospects and referral-request dialogues with clients are plentiful. However, be discerning in what you choose to say. Some of the verbiage advisors are encouraged to try makes me cringe. I've seen suggestions that advisors ask their top clients face-to-face if they're finding the service and advice that the advisor is providing helpful and timely. The idea is that if the client says yes, then the advisor can suggest that surely they'd want their friends and family helped in the same way and then can ask for names and contact details. To me, this is a total setup and feels like a strong-arm sales technique. As a producing advisor myself, I would never want to back my clients into a corner like this. In fact, there is no way I'd say much of what I've read because I know that not only would those approaches not succeed with my clients but would also turn them off.

If something feels stiff or uncomfortable for you to say, don't say it. Be natural and genuine. Slick pitches and stiff scripts will, at best, result in an "I'll think about it," which is usually just a polite way for people to say no when they feel uncomfortable. You don't want to say words that are going to potentially alienate a good client by making them feel they are being sold to or used. Practice words that feel normal and relaxed, words that you would feel comfortable using again and again.

Some people object to using rehearsed words as being canned or contrived. They say that if someone asks, you should spontaneously and instinctively explain what you do so it sounds authentic. But, if you don't have some preplanned, practiced words to briefly communicate what you do in a clear, concise, and compelling manner, you'll likely lose the opportunity for deeper conversation. At a cocktail party or networking function, the reality is that you have only a few seconds to capture someone's attention. People are constantly being bombarded by sound bites, each vying for their attention. You have competition, so you need to be prepared to ensure what you say will be heard above the noise. When you are succinct, confident, and relaxed, you're memorable. That's highly unlikely to happen if you're trying to come up with a spontaneous response.

Don't worry, and don't tie yourself up in knots over this. Also, don't sell yourself short or use the excuse that planning what you'll say in advance is just not your style. Coaching clients tell me that role-playing conversations is one of the most transformative and empowering things we do in our sessions together. By planning and practicing what to say, I have seen extremely introverted advisors grow in confidence and actually come to enjoy the opportunity to talk with people they don't know. They can't wait to find out if the person they are speaking with might need their help and be a perfect fit for their business.

Learned, rehearsed words can be delivered genuinely and believably. In fact, practicing lets you get comfortable with how the words sound coming out of your mouth. But don't fool yourself into thinking you're ready because you've practiced the words you want to say in your head. Words can look great on paper or in your mind, but the first time you say them out loud, you'll probably trip over them. That's normal. Keep practicing out loud. Play with your cadence, tone, and inflection. Get used to how the words feel to say and how they sound. You're going to be saying these words out loud to real people—make them work for you. Practicing doesn't mean you're going to be acting; be your genuine self— your *prepared* genuine self.

GIVE THEM WHAT THEY WANT

The people you are talking with deserve your very best, most precise, articulate explanation of how you can help them and why they should work with you. By planning and practicing the words you want to say ahead of time, you'll make sure you're clear and don't waste their time with waffling. When I'm on stage speaking, I don't go on about how wonderful it is to be there and thank the audience for having me before I start into my content. Those words might sound ingratiating, but they're fluff because they don't get to what the audience wants to hear: solutions to their issues and information about how to be more effective at what they do. When I begin, I use words that I have carefully chosen and specifically practiced so that I grab their attention and start providing value right away. Your clients and prospects most want to know how they will benefit from working with you; choose words that get right to the point and provide the information they want. (See Figure 5.1.)

REAL-LIFE CONVERSATIONS

Here are some examples of different situations and effective, real-life conversations with explanations of why these words work. Use them to craft and practice your own questions and responses.

Prospecting at Social Functions

Unlike most people you'll meet at social events, you don't have to be nervous about what you'll say in conversations with people you don't know. You can relax because you will be prepared and will have practiced how to guide your conversations.

Avoid closed-ended questions that lead directly to yes or no answers. If you're trying to find out how this person is related to your host Brian, questions like, "Do you work with Brian?" or, "Are you friends with Brian?"

KEYS TO EFFECTIVE CONVERSATIONS

You've met someone at a social or business event. After the initial introductions, what do you say next?

- **Focus on the other person.** This isn't an inquisition; however, make it your mission to find out as much as you can about them.

- **Don't ask, "What do you do?"** They likely "do" lots of things. Asking good questions will allow you to discover what they do to earn income, if that's what you want to know.

- **Ask open-ended questions.** Questions that require more than a yes or no answer will give you more information about the other person. Use words like *how, why, where,* and *what.*

- **Wait for people to finish their thought or story.** Before you jump in with what you have to say, allow the other person to complete what he or she has to say.

- **Be genuinely interested in what they have to say.** Listen for snippets of information you can use to ask further questions. "Tell me more about…"

- **Don't worry about impressing them with your accomplishments.** Answer their questions about you, but then continue asking questions about them. They'll get to know you more as your relationship progresses.

Figure 5.1

are likely to generate quick, one-word responses that won't reveal much. You'll be left mentally scurrying for what to say next. Instead, ask *how* or *where* questions that require the responder to give more information. "*How* do you know Brian?" "*How* long have you known him?" "*Where* did you meet him?"

Here is a sample dialogue with a man and a woman standing together at Brian and Jill's wedding being held in San Francisco. You've traded introductions with the man, Bruce, who is not a natural chatterbox. He might be shy, tired, just not enjoy weddings, or all of these. People like this may be more of a challenge to continue talking with, but you can see how it's possible to move the conversation along.

You: "How do you know Brian and Jill?"

Bruce: "Brian and I went to school together."

You: "Oh, really; where was that?"

Bruce: "Minnesota."

You: "Oh wow, that's a ways away. Are you out here for the wedding or do you live out here now?"

Bruce: "We live out here."

Notice you've used *how* and *where* questions to find out more information so you can continue with more questions to progress the conversation, even with someone who isn't very expressive. If you're paying attention to his answers, you'll be thinking about the significant difference between property prices in Minnesota and the San Francisco Bay Area. Perhaps they have significant money that enabled the move, or maybe they're financially stretched and good candidates for some financial planning.

At this point, resist the inclination to ask what I call "The Question of Death": "What do you do?" It's a lazy way to get to know people and implies the most significant thing about them is their job, which may be only a small part of the picture you want to learn about. They may not even have a job, or the answer may be a curt and uninformative, "Lots of stuff." If this is one of your first questions, it might kill the conversation before it ever really gets started. You can find out what work they do in the course of your conversation, but ask questions that reveal much more as well.

You: "So, Bruce, what brought you out to the Bay Area?"

Bruce: "Career decision. My wife, Mary, came out here to go to law school."

Mentally, you're noting that law can be a lucrative career. You want to know more: Is she a lawyer or did she used to be? Is he a lawyer? They might be interesting prospects, but again, don't jump to the questions about jobs. Find out more about them as people first. You now have information to easily include her in the conversation.

You: "What law school did you go to, Mary?"

Mary: "Boalt, at Berkeley. I studied real estate law."

You: "Oh, what did you end up doing with that?"

You'll likely find out some of her professional history, more details about her interests, and what she is doing now. She'll probably tell you what her studies led her to, or that she didn't enjoy it and left law behind to pursue other interests. Whatever her answers, you'll have plenty to keep you going on your mission to gather as much important information as you can.

You: "So, did you stay in Berkeley after law school or move elsewhere?"

You may find out more about where she works or what he does for work if they moved to be closer to employers.

Mary: "We were living in Oakland while I was in school, but we wanted someplace quieter and with better schools. We live down in Palo Alto now."

Alarm bells should be going off as you make your mental notes: schools mean children, college savings, and possibly one income at some point.

You: "So schools...you have children?"

Mary: "We have twin girls and a son."

You: "Oh. How old are they?"

Up until this point, you haven't told them what you do, yet you're finding out a load of important information about them.

While I've told you to avoid asking "The Question of Death," undoubtedly people will ask you what you do. If you have been able to take the time to find out what issues concern the person you're dialoging with, you can tailor your response to their interests. In this scenario, you might answer, "I'm a financial advisor, helping people plan and avoid mistakes. I work with a number of families figuring out what funding college education looks like."

In this instance, you don't need to talk any further about you, what you think, or what you do; instead, get back to them. At this point in a conversation, people often assume you're about to pitch your services to them. And you are...just not the way they're expecting.

You: "What do you and the kids think about the schools in your area? Any ideas about college yet?"

Now you're showing Mary and Bruce you're genuinely interested in them as a family and not just in what you can get from them. Internally, you might be jumping up and down at the possibility of them becoming clients, but resist appearing too eager at this point. Be disciplined as you position yourself as a scarce commodity, not desperate to do business with just anyone, even if you're at the point in your business where you'll talk with anyone who will listen in an effort to meet your client-quota numbers.

When you don't overtly try to sell yourself upon meeting new people, an interesting psychological process can happen. Almost everyone naturally wants to be liked and seen as desirable. By holding off trying to win over prospects, they will likely begin to wonder why you're not trying to impress them. You may find they start plying you with questions as the roles reverse and they actively attempt to appeal to you. Don't be surprised to see this happen when you meet new prospects.

As they ask questions about you, be prepared to give away some of your expertise and offer helpful information to give them a taste of how you work with people. Most people are eager to talk about their children, and asking questions related to them is often a quick way to find out all sorts of information about the family's interests and plans for the future. Ask about potential college interests and mention how you are helping clients deal with continually rising education costs. Perhaps you are helping clients explore nontraditional ways to structure 529 plans or alternative ways to save funds for college costs.

Look for ways to compliment smart decisions. Mary's possibly earning a high income. Ask if her firm has a 401(k) and whether she maxes out her contribution.

You: "That's great that you're maxing that out, especially if the company is providing a match. Not doing that is really leaving money on the table."

Then, you can subtly show a little more depth.

You: "Some people overlook that you can actually contribute more than that, possibly even $18,000. And once you get to age 50, you can even contribute an additional $6,000. So, from a tax perspective that means you can considerably reduce your reportable earnings. They're appealing options to consider." (Note: These figures are the 2015 employee elective deferral limits.)

If they want to go deeper than this, your response is simple.

You: "Sure, I'd love to talk with you more. I also have some helpful information on college savings I could email you, if you like. Do you have a card or contact email I can get?"

Or, for a really confident approach give them your card.

You: "Here's my card. I'm sure with three youngsters, you keep busy. Whenever you'd like to set up a time to grab a coffee and talk further, shoot me an email with some times and days that work for you."

Then, simply finish the conversation.

You: "Sounds like they're getting ready to cut the cake. I think I'll head over there."

There's been nothing needy, desperate, overbearing, or threatening from you. Will they be one of your 15? You don't know yet, but the point is you've given yourself the opportunity to step closer to achieving your goal. Pat yourself on the back and move forward.

Prospecting in an Elevator

If you get asked, "What do you do?" and only have seconds to give a strong response—without any background information about the person asking you the question—you can still be compelling without sounding desperate or cheesy. You might answer, "I'm a financial advisor and help people with answers to questions that keep them up at night, about things like college education costs, plans for retirement, and selling a business." Note that you haven't mentioned anything about beating the market or investment returns, but you've been specific about the value you bring to your clients.

Alternatively, you might want to answer by asking a question of your own.

Prospect: "What do you do?"

You: "I'm a financial advisor. I help people answer the questions and manage the concerns that keep them up at night; it's kind of a counseling role. Do you mind if I ask you a question?"

Prospect: "Sure."

You: "I'm always interested to hear what's on people's minds. If I asked you what your main financial concern or question was, what would you say?"

Note that framing rather personal questions in this hypothetical way invites people to safely reveal more than they typically would if you asked the question directly. They are only telling you what they would say *if* you asked the question, rather than feeling like they're being directly asked something quite personal. It's a subtle but significant difference and a useful technique to apply in many exploratory discussions.

When they tell you their answer and it relates to what you offer, you can reply that you help clients figure out answers to their concerns about the very same things. You can hand them your card and say, "If you'd like to discuss this further, or you have other financial questions, give me a call. I'd be happy to help you where I can." If they don't want to reveal their concerns to you then and there, you can mention something that has broad interest and seems likely to relate to them, such as, "Well, a lot of people have questions about retirement or Social Security and want to know, 'Do I have enough saved to get me through retirement?' or

'When should I start collecting Social Security?' I help with issues like that. If you have any concerns about how those things might play out for you, give me call. I'd be happy to answer any questions you might have." Either way, you can move on, leaving the ball in their court. And, you haven't come across as desperate or pushy, but instead have shown you're helpful and confident.

Prospecting by Cold-Walking

Cold-walking is a lot like cold-calling, but you actually get out in your neighborhood and start pounding the pavement. It can be a great way to show prospects you're local and convenient to meet with. Even if they have a relationship with another advisor elsewhere, the fact that you are a part of their community can be a strong benefit in your favor.

When I began working as an advisor, I got my first client by cold-walking. I walked down three blocks and stepped into a dental office. The owner was in the reception area, and all I said was the following:

My name is Paul Kingsman, and I work down the road at Morgan Stanley. Just wanted to pop in and say, "Hi." I've owned my own business and know the challenges that come with it, such as staffing and payroll. Whenever you have 15 minutes for a coffee, if you'd like to talk further, here's my card.

After looking around the waiting room and seeing the books and toys for children, I added, "Nice waiting room, by the way. I bet the toys are a big hit!"

His next words were, "Actually, do you have a minute now?" From there, we began talking. I had given him the option to take my card, say thanks, and have that be the last he saw of me. Instead, he said the timing couldn't have been better because he had some questions about "all that stuff." My business partner and I met with him and his wife, and we began a great relationship.

There are a few key things to remember if you're going to walk into someone's business. Keep in mind that this is their place of business, so they call the shots:

- If they have a No Solicitation sign out front, respect them and their rules.

- Be aware of their time. I walked into the dentist's office about 4:45 in the afternoon, close to when I thought he'd be finished with patients for the day and I would not be an annoying distraction. If there had been someone waiting, I would have asked his receptionist for a card, mentioned I would send Steve, the dentist, an email letting him know I came by, and then left.

- Prepare ahead for your visits by doing some online research about the company and the owners to determine possible points of connection and how you might be able to help them.

- Keep your words to a concise introduction. The last thing a busy business owner wants is someone who doesn't know when to end the conversation and leave. If they take your card and simply say thanks and nothing more, take that as your cue to move on.

- Notice special things they are doing to promote their business or connect with their customers that you can compliment, showing you are aware of the effort it takes to attract customers and cultivate loyalty.

Don't try to close a deal then and there. This is not the place or time, and you don't yet know enough about them to definitively determine if they are a good fit for your business. Your main aim is to add people to your list of viable prospects. You could say, "If you have any questions about retirement stuff, education funding, or just what's happening out there in the economy or market, here's my card. Feel free to send me an email. I'd be more than happy to answer your questions or send you some helpful information." You never know what people have going on, and showing them that you're thoughtful and helpful, even when there might not be anything in it for you, makes a bigger positive impression than simply telling them what you do. Be patient, helpful, and aware.

Prospecting with People Who Aren't Ready to Commit

Perhaps you reach the end of an exploratory meeting with a prospect, and while they appear to be a good fit and seem interested, they aren't quite ready to commit then and there. Don't try to pressure them into making a decision they're not ready to make. You only want clients who are happy to follow your direction, so don't start the relationship by pushing them. Let them know you have a procedure for what will happen next if they decide to work with you.

> You: "From what you've shared, it seems like I'd be able to help with what you've got going on. I'll send you a summary of what we discussed and what the next steps might look like if we end up working together. Think about it for a few days and let me know what you think. The decision to move forward or not will be up to you."

You can follow up with a phone call if you don't hear from them after a week. Ask if they have any more questions and whether they have made a decision about how they would like to proceed. If they want to come on board, continue with your process. If they say they are still thinking about it or have decided not to proceed, be confident in your process and thank them for considering you. Keep going back to the fact that you're looking for your *perfect* 15 people, and that includes those with a willing attitude. Don't waste a moment arm wrestling people.

ADDRESSING THE ELEPHANT IN THE ROOM

Often, new advisors I've worked with are so nervous about being asked how long they've been in the industry and not having a "good" answer that they tend to avoid prospecting conversations all together. That makes it tough to build your business.

Being prepared means also being realistic, and questions (verbalized or not) about your longevity in the industry are bound to come up, especially if you look young. Seasoned businesspeople, in particular, know the value of experience and will typically want to know more about you before they trust you further. "How long have you been an advisor?" stems from their bigger, unstated question, "Why should I trust you?" You need to anticipate the question and be prepared so you can answer it without seeming embarrassed, making excuses, rushing past their reasonable query, or otherwise seeming to try to hide your lack of tenure.

First, consider the question in the context of the whole conversation with a prospect. Perhaps you meet potential clients through a mutual friend's housewarming party. As illustrated in the dialogues above, keep the first conversation focused on them, asking plenty of questions and genuinely listening to their answers. Keep any talk about what you do brief at this initial stage, and highlight how you help people. If they seem like they might be a good prospect and express interest in knowing more about what you do, invite them to meet for a coffee to get to know more about each other.

When you meet, continue asking questions about them. Perhaps by this stage you know what they do for work. Ask them what attracted them to their field and what they like most about what they do. How do they help their clients? Listen for points of connection and share some of your background to demonstrate your expertise. Point out similar values or motivation you share to help make connections.

Concentrate your discussion on areas you've learned are important to them, such as getting a child through college without going broke, knowing the best things to do with money they're saving for retirement, preparing to pay for care for an aging parent, or how to make sure they don't outlive their own money. Emphasize the value you bring to your relationships with clients and touch on your process.

"So many people allocate little time to planning for the longer term, but there's so much happening that really impacts their financial well-being, both now and down the road. Helping people understand how a healthcare event can impact them or their family, or to make solid decisions about how to prepare for college costs that typically are rising by more than 5 percent each year, or determine the most strategic time to tap into Social Security so they don't leave scads of cash on the table… those are all reasons I love being an advisor. I really enjoy helping people make sound decisions that will make a positive difference in their and their loved ones' lives.

"Sometimes I meet people who just want to talk about picking stocks or discuss market movements. And while I do keep a perspective on the markets and know about the current 10-year Treasury yield and interest rates, as well as how various global events are affecting the financial world, monitoring portfolio performance is just one small part of what I do. It is only one piece of the puzzle when I help families and individuals plan wisely given their current financial situation and what they want things to look like later. I know those folks who are most concerned with daily fluctuations of individual stocks aren't a good fit for the way I do business and so quickly encourage them to save their money and get an online account where they can easily monitor the markets and do trades themselves.

"When I work with new clients I want to know their financial concerns, challenges, and goals. I enjoy getting a view of their overall picture because I can see how they are tracking toward their longer-term objectives or make a sound plan to get them where they want to be. I help my clients do things like be aware of their personal balance sheet, manage their cash flow, ensure they have a realistic emergency fund in plain old boring cash, consider appropriate insurance, and make sure their estate is in order—all key financial health issues."

If and when the question, "How long have you been in the industry?" does come, you will have already demonstrated your professional, thoughtful approach to your relationships with your clients and the service you provide them. This question is just a small element in a broader conversation that has, by this stage, presented many compelling answers to the underlying question of, "Why should I trust you?" So, go ahead and answer the question calmly and confidently: "I finally began earlier this year [or whatever time frame is appropriate for your situation]." Phrasing it this way with the word *finally* communicates that you do have relevant experience for the position you're in, even though your time as an officially licensed advisor may be relatively short.

Then in a warm, relaxed tone give them a little background.

"I've seen people make some less-than-wise financial decisions and then watched the sad consequences unfold. I want to help people avoid the same mistakes I've seen others make. I've known for a long time that this was what I wanted to do, and I love helping people successfully reach their financial objectives."

Or, "I've always loved helping people solve problems, and that's what I do now" or, "I've always really enjoyed explaining complicated topics in ways that people can easily understand and then help them use that knowledge to discover new possibilities for their own lives." If you've had another career before becoming an advisor, draw a connection about how your previous experience makes you a stronger advisor. You don't need to be nervous or make excuses, just continue the conversation with poise. You might have butterflies in your stomach, but deliver your words assuredly, just as you have practiced and prepared to do.

Everyone in this business has a starting point. It takes time to build industry experience, but the sooner you get started meeting and talking to people, the sooner your confidence will grow and the more consistent your prospecting results will be. Keep reminding yourself that you are looking for your specific number of right clients who are a good fit for you and your business. If your lack of years as an advisor is the reason a prospect doesn't want to work with you, that's fine; they're not a good fit. You'll know you've given them plenty of other reasons why clients can trust you and explanations of real value and help you provide people who do choose to work with you.

ASKING FOR REFERRALS

With clients who love how you help them, asking for referrals becomes anxiety-free. How and when you ask are key to everyone's comfort and your success in getting what you want. A great time to discuss referrals is when you have just answered their questions or addressed concerns they have brought to you. When they have recently experienced the value you provide, it's no great effort to suggest they encourage their contacts to have the same reassuring experience.

You: "You know, if your friends or family have any questions like this or regarding what's happening in the markets, or if they want to learn a little more about how they can effectively plan for their financial future, have them call me. I'd be happy to talk with them for a few minutes. I can't promise I'll bring them on as clients, unless it's a great fit for us both. But I'd be happy to spend a little time answering questions they have."

This phrasing is powerful and can be your default way to ask for referrals. Let's break it down and see what makes it work.

"…if your friends or family have any questions like this or regarding what's happening in the markets, or if they want to learn a little more about how they can effectively plan for their financial future, have them call me."

First, you highlight that you're interested in what's important to them: helping their family and friends. And, by inviting them to call you, you clarify that you're not going to impose on or hound them. Be confident that if they're really interested, they'll call.

"I'd be happy to talk with them for a few minutes."

Note that you want to talk *with* people, not talk *to* them (which implies talking *at* them, and you definitely do not want to do that). Your client already knows you have had informative, helpful conversations with them, and that's what you're offering to people they care about. You communicate that you're pleased to converse with them, learn more about them, and try to help them, without trying to sell them or force them into anything. You also indicate that you are not expecting to spend a great deal of your time or theirs—this will be a brief conversation, unless you both agree there is value in talking further.

"I can't promise I'll bring them on as clients, unless it's a great fit for us both."

This is a key line. If their Uncle Larry wants to trade Facebook stock all day or hunt for the next hot IPO, he's not a good fit for you. You've clearly given yourself a way out with little risk of offending your client. More important, you've shown your client you're discerning about who you work with. It's a subtle way to elevate the service you provide without grabbing the spotlight and shining it on yourself. Finally, you've indirectly sent the message to your client that he or she is a great fit for you, and vice versa. This deepens your client relationships, and they feel good because they know you value them and they are privileged to be in your select fold of clients.

This dialogue is particularly useful because you can repeat it over and over. If you hold quarterly reviews for your best clients, you can use this key line as often as every other meeting. More than likely, they'll mention friends or family in the course of the conversation, and you can be ready with a request for a referral that is shaped as a generous offer to help. Many lines I've seen suggested elsewhere are only good for one-time use. For referrals you want a format that you can use constantly and that doesn't make you sound desperate. You run a high risk of putting your clients on the spot if you directly ask them to tell you how you have helped them, when your real aim is getting them to give you names of other people to prospect. You need to earn the right to expect referrals, and if you work diligently and provide value enough to do that, chances are the referrals will come your way simply by doing what you do best: helping people.

DISTRACTION-PROOF STEPS

1. Know what you're going to say.

2. Practice so it sounds and feels natural.

3. Listen thoroughly.

4. Respond clearly, conversationally, and with conviction.

By knowing what to say, and just as important, how and when to say it, you'll go from simply talking to becoming a great communicator. Develop an approach that feels comfortable and natural. Be prepared to talk with anyone, because you never know when and where you might find that right person to fill one of your available spots.

People need your help making some of their most important decisions; be confident about your ability to do this and know you don't have to hard-sell people to convince them of what you can do. This will likely take time, and you may even make mistakes as you get comfortable with what to say and how to deliver it. Keep engaging; this is a people-oriented business, and you're still looking for your right number of ideal clients. In the next chapter, we'll talk about what to do with your right clients once you find them.

CHAPTER SIX

FOCUS ON THE RIGHT CLIENTS

"Setting a goal is not the main thing. It is deciding how you will go about achieving it and staying with that plan."

– TOM LANDRY, FOOTBALL PLAYER AND COACH

I f you don't have an effective system to segment and appropriately service clients, you'll be distracted by:

- Clients who want to monopolize your time and energy, yet provide very little in return

- Worrying about important actions falling through the gaps in your servicing process

- Reacting to client demands instead of implementing planned service activities

Time is your most valuable resource, and it's not renewable—once it's gone, you can't get it back. How much do you value your time? Are you conscious about how you allocate your time? Everyone has the same number of hours each day, but how and where you use your time will determine the return you enjoy on the time you spend. Are you using your time in ways that effectively move you toward that vivid picture you created at the beginning of this process?

You want to demonstrate that you take care of your clients. While all of them should always receive great service from you, their frequency of contact with you will vary, if you want to keep your sanity. There will be clients you should spend more time with and those who don't get to engage with you as often because they provide a smaller return to your business. This chapter will provide you with an effective way to structure your book and establish a strategic routine to ensure you connect with all of your clients in degrees proportionate to their value to your business.

Ironman triathlons are Herculean efforts: after swimming 2.4 miles and biking 112 miles, competitors get to run a marathon—all in one day! I've coached a number of Ironman athletes in their swimming, and without exception, when each person started working with me their plan was to complete the swimming leg of the race as fast as possible. However, that first segment of the race is the shortest; the 2.4-mile swim is relatively less demanding than the bike ride or run, taking only about 90 minutes of the 10+-hour event. The best competitors actually conserve their energy on the swim and don't even start kicking until about 100 yards from the finish. It takes self-control to stick to their race plan and to keep that activity in perspective relative to the requirements of the long day. They might not be the first ones out of the water, but they complete the swim having preserved their legs for the upcoming ride and run. If they give the swim everything they have, they might gain an advantage of 10 minutes over other competitors, but at what cost? They will have already started accumulating lactic acid in their legs and may not even be able to finish the marathon. Those 10 minutes gained will quickly slip away later in the day because they spent their valuable energy on an activity that provided relatively little return. All competitors must complete the swim, but the most successful will conserve their limited energy to expend it in the marathon, when a little extra effort can provide a much bigger payoff.

Like an Ironman race, building your advisory business is a huge task and requires your commitment over a long haul. You have a lot of different activities that must be done, but not all of them provide equal returns. When advisors are new to the business, they tend to provide all their clients their best effort and give as much time as a client wants, much like the triathletes who wanted to give 100 percent effort to every part of their race. They reason that they show clients how much they care by spending time with them, but as their businesses grow they soon find they do not have enough time or energy to spend equally with all of the people on their growing client roster. Their original clients, who tend to become smaller clients as time goes on, get used to the advisor's highest level of service and come to expect a lot of attention for comparatively little return for the advisor, who ends up feeling frazzled because there never seems to be enough time to get everything done.

That's exactly what happened to Susan. She was always quick to respond to every request of a vocal client with $150,000, and over the years that client developed the habit of calling every Tuesday morning and expecting half an hour of her time to chat about the latest market commentary he heard on CNBC. At the same time, Susan's business was growing and she had a lot to do. She was starting to resent the Tuesday morning calls, which made her feel like she was running behind schedule the rest of the day. She knew she needed to touch base with a quiet client with $1.5 million, but the call kept getting pushed down her to-do list because of the other demands on her time. Before she knew it, Susan hadn't spoken with one of her largest and most valuable clients in more than six months. She began to feel she was never quite in control of her business and was spending a lot of energy worrying that it wasn't as profitable as she'd like.

Susan's $150,000 client was thrilled and loved her, but he only provided her about $1,500 a year in fees. While Susan assumed her $1.5 million client was content because she was quiet, the client actually felt like she rarely heard from Susan and wondered if anyone was really paying attention to her money. She's thought about shopping for another advisor, putting her $15,000 annual management fee to Susan at risk. If Susan spent half an hour a week with her smaller client, by default the value of that time would be approximately $60 per hour ($1,500 ÷ [0.5 hour × 50 weeks] = $60 per hour). If she spent only one hour each quarter with her larger client, that time would be worth $3,750 per hour ($15,000 ÷ [1 hour × 4 quarters] = $3,750 per hour). It's not hard to see where Susan should have been allocating her time to secure the greatest return.

Are you recognizing your larger clients' value to your business? Do you conserve energy with your smaller clients so you have a bit extra to give to your larger clients, where a little extra effort will have a big payoff? Or do you spend just as much of your valuable, limited time on smaller clients, giving them the same level of attention as your largest clients? Those vocal small clients probably like you, and it feels great to be liked, but is that warm feeling costing you progress toward your bigger-picture objective? Maybe you're not aware of budding dissatisfaction and cooler feelings from larger clients just because they are quiet. Warm feelings from happy larger clients are much more profitable.

Keep in mind that care and attention are two different things. You should thoroughly care for *all* of your clients, from your largest (with the great assets, multiple family accounts, and complex trust needs) to an individual with a small IRA rollover. Clients' asset levels should never affect how much you respect them and want to help them. Your concern for all your clients should be identical. In fact, you have equal fiduciary responsibility to all of them: you need to know what investments they have in their accounts, why they're there, and what role they play in their overall portfolio performance, regardless of the size of their assets. But the time you allocate to them and the attention you give them must differ. Larger clients merit more of your attention because they bring more value to your business. You want to ensure they are happy with your service so that you gain their confidence and earn referrals to more folks like them. You will still care for your smaller clients, but be sure the attention they receive from you is commensurate with the value they are bringing to your business.

In previous chapters, we learned that business growth does not necessarily equal business success. If you grow an unwieldy business, with a broad range of investments and products to monitor and no clear structure, you will create significant problems for yourself. When it comes to their money, clients can quickly become disgruntled if they feel like they are being ignored or important details of their financial well-being are being overlooked. If you have a structure that allows you to monitor and review clients' situations quickly yet thoroughly, it will ensure that all their expectations are being met. Carefully establishing your limited variety of investment models, as we've already covered, is a good first step that will allow you to create a scalable platform for growing a manageable business. It's also important to find a way to manage the time you spend servicing your clients, ensuring that they all receive equal care from you with appropriate levels of attention. Don't devote the same amount of your time to someone who generates $1,000 a year for you as you devote to someone who spends $10,000 a year.

The basis of an effective client servicing process is a consistent, uniform fee structure that is applied to clients who are invested in your core models. How are you deriving your revenue, who is it coming from, and how much of your time will it take to generate it? If you know the answers to these questions, tracking this information will be simple. A uniform fee structure allows this to happen—plus it's transparent. As you start analyzing this area of your business, you may realize the fees you're charging are not consistent, especially if you've inherited clients from other advisors. If you continue to charge new clients different fees for the same products and services, pulling your revenue data together will be cumbersome and more time-consuming, and you'll probably avoid doing it. Without the data, your business projections will be based only on guesses and broad assumptions. However, by being aware of the need to standardize this key element of your business, you can introduce a set fee structure for new clients and ensure increasing fee consistency over time.

Don't be tempted to offer discounts to meet prices new clients previously received from other advisors. If they're talking about leaving another advisor to work with you, chances are their decision to move has nothing to do with fees. Clearly and unapologetically tell new clients your fee structure, and then move on. Consistent fees make realistic business revenue projections simple, which make decisions about expansion like hiring a new advisor or growing into new premises less risky. Also, this consistency frees you to focus on your most important roles: servicing existing clients and finding new ones.

Next, rank clients by the revenue they generate, from greatest to least. Compare this to a list of your clients ranked by AUM. The rankings on these two lists should be comparable. If you find great disparities, figure out what's causing the differences. For example, did a client with smaller assets purchase an annuity that generated fees, kicking up their revenue ranking over the past 12 months? This information is key to being a proactive business owner. Review these figures at least annually to ensure you know who your most profitable clients are. You want to give them the superior service they deserve so that you spend your time cost-effectively. Some advisors analyze their revenue sources quarterly, and as you grow, if you have efficient systems set up, you might like to do it that often, too. However, don't spend inordinate amounts of time on this, because it is simply a tool to implement your next step: sorting your clients into different service levels.

A simple tiered service structure will allow you to pay appropriate attention to both your largest revenue-generating clients and your less profitable clients. You will be able to rest easy, knowing you've achieved the following:

- *Recognizing who your biggest clients are and providing them outstanding service.* Don't assume your most valuable clients will automatically get your best service. As your business grows, you'll get busier. Unless they are deliberately planned, activities that you want to do for clients will slip between the cracks, and you'll miss opportunities to do things that could lead to great impressions and valuable referrals.

- *Knowing exactly who you should focus on next.* You can preplan the service you provide, so your clients know they can trust you to provide timely advice. You'll avoid living in reaction mode, having your days driven by whoever is concerned or irritated about an issue enough to finally call you. With consistent procedures in place, you and your staff will be clear about the deliverables you provide clients, with nothing left to chance.

- *Knowing when you need help.* Because you will be consciously allocating time for portfolio reviews and other servicing activities, you'll be able to see more clearly whether your feelings of being overwhelmed can be reduced by simply avoiding unproductive distractions or are really due to the fact that you're at capacity. You will always allocate the majority of your time to your largest clients, but when you start finding it challenging to effectively service your C and D clients because of lack of time, you can make informed decisions about hiring a junior advisor to take care of these clients.

- *Seeing common concerns your top clients share and maximizing solutions.* As you deepen your relationships with your highest value clients, you'll become more proficient at recognizing and proactively addressing their needs. You'll notice they face similar issues, and when you find solutions for one you'll be able to maximize your effort by duplicating those solutions for others who have the same concerns.

- *Focusing on finding more top-tier clients.* As you maintain your approach to this client level, their growing trust will lead to more referrals. Your consistent focus on higher value prospects will make you more aware of issues important to them, so you'll be better prepared to connect with them and communicate how you help people like them.

- *Identifying clients who tend to take a lot of your time yet produce very little revenue.* Maintain perspective on your business: value your time, effort, and advice and make sure you're being compensated for it. You need to have these clients adhere to your business structure or ask them to find an advisor who is a better fit.

At your onboarding meetings with new clients, clearly communicate the service they will receive from you. How often will they hear from you and meet with you? Will they always communicate directly with you, or will they be interacting with others who are a part of your business? Your deliverables will differ depending on the client's asset size and needs. Effectively manage their expectations. Some advisors express concern at treating clients differently from one another, but remember that they won't be aware that you have differing levels of service. They'll just know that you consistently deliver exactly what you've promised. You know you have a scalable, manageable business system that ensures it.

While the end result of creating different service levels is the same, how you'll get there depends on what stage you're at in building your business. Typically, advisors I work with are at one of three stages when we begin together. The first are those who are starting their businesses from scratch: they're fresh from their first round of company training, still getting to know their way around their forms gallery, and now are faced with the reality of building a business. These advisors are excited and seem optimistic, but many struggle with whether or not they can actually do it. If this is you, you are not alone! (We'll address this concern in Chapter 9.)

Advisors in the second group have been in the business for between two and five years. Typically, they were handed lower-tier clients from other advisors in their office at the insistence of their office manager or picked up clients from advisors who have left their firm. They have some idea of how they should grow their business, but they also have a wild spread of client assets and an unwieldy mix of investments. They know they need a structure to manage what they presently have and also allow for growth. They have a vision for what they can achieve but need some help with creating and implementing a scalable business structure that will allow effective ways to both service their current clients and bring in new business. While people in the first group are knowledgeable but anxious, people in this second group are usually knowledgeable and frustrated.

People in the third group have been in the industry for six years or longer, have gathered a good AUM base, but cannot grow much further because they are limited by their structure. They have permitted growth to happen randomly. While they planned to move new clients' investments into their models and even told new clients they would review their holdings once their ACATs arrived, for a variety of reasons no investment changes were ever made. While sounding like they were being accommodating, these advisors only made their jobs more difficult with each new client. They now have a huge range of mutual funds, ETFs, and individual stocks that they struggle to monitor, putting both their clients and themselves in a risky situation. They've seen enough of this business to know they have painted themselves into a corner and need help. Their businesses used to be much more fun, and they desperately want to get back the lost feelings of control. They wish they could return to growing their businesses and providing exceptional service to clients who want to work with them, but because they are operating at capacity they just feel too busy to try doing anything differently.

See if you recognize yourself or your own business in the following examples.

STAGE ONE: STARTING OUT

Sarah wanted to be in the financial services industry since college. She read a lot about different investment styles and financial planning processes while studying for her Series 7. She passed her exam and returned home from her first stint of company training. With her progress being monitored closely by her office manager and the national sales manager, she was understandably a little nervous when she was starting out. She had heard how she should be looking to onboard anyone with a pulse (though that approach had never sat well with her), had a short list of family she was going to approach for business, and was scanning her LinkedIn connections for decent prospects. She had practiced how to get into effective prospecting conversations and was ready to proceed with bringing on clients. Spending significant time and focus on a segmented service structure was not a top priority for Sarah at the start because she did not yet have any clients to provide different levels of service to. However, she was wisely aware of the importance of having a structure and so began to formulate what different service levels might look like based on potential client sizes and needs.

One of Sarah's TARGET Goals was to bring in $10 million of new assets within her first year. She was specific about how many people that meant and what assets they needed:

- 6 clients with $500,000+ of assets to manage ($3MM+)

- 16 clients with between $250,000 and $499,999 of assets to manage (with an average of $300,000 = $4.8MM+)

- 15 clients with between $100,000 and $249,000 of assets to manage (with an average of $150,000 = $2.25MM+)

- Total: 37 new clients with $10+ million of assets to manage

Sarah's personal numbers differed from the sample presented in Chapter 4, but her format was the same. She needed to gain some confidence. She had a helpful office manager, and with the payout she was on she felt she could grow from these numbers once she had a year's experience under her belt. Getting her first half-million-dollar clients felt challenging, but achievable. Most important, Sarah started out keeping score: she knew exactly who she was looking for. She had also chosen an appropriate client service model and matrix of deliverables, which we'll see in more detail shortly. Because she was just beginning, the restrictions of her system were somewhat fluid, but she had a framework in place for servicing her clients.

For the sake of her long-term business growth, Sarah recognized the need to see herself as a financial advisor rather than an investment manager. She saw the importance of presenting a finite offering of investment choices for incoming clients, and accepted that spending excessive time trying to figure out how to beat market returns would, based on historical data, only waste time and ultimately dilute her focus. She was determined to assemble and stick to several asset-allocated mutual fund and ETF models for her clients. She knew that as her business grew she might consider speaking with a few third-party asset managers to discuss their investment strategies and incorporate some different offerings in her mix. However, for the time being, she decided she would not be distracted by considering many different investment options: she wanted to find her new clients and build the business she had in mind as quickly as she could.

To start, Sarah separated her potential clients into three groups:

- $500,000 and above would be her A client group.

- $250,000 to $499,999 would be her B clients.

- $100,000 to $249,000 would be her C clients.

She didn't agonize over deciding on the breakpoints for these levels; she knew they were flexible and could be altered as she went along. These groupings simply provided her with benchmarks to guide her in sorting and servicing her new clients. These classifications were only for her use, and clients didn't know that they were in tiered groups. Sarah knew she would eventually want to add a D group, but while she was getting started that could wait. She realized that some of her initial C clients would eventually be classed as D clients. They wouldn't know or feel much difference in service when that change came, but Sarah strategically gave herself some space in her book and schedule to grow.

It can be tempting to feel like your first clients are all A clients because they are your only clients. However, more clients will be coming—and soon. Walk and talk as though you have them now. Expect that your business will thrive. When it does start growing, you'll be happy you established your tiered structure and committed to it. For Sarah, her first client had $378,600, and so he was a B client. She gave him great service, but she understood and remembered he was a B client. She kept her primary focus on finding her A clients and so resisted overservicing her new B client. Following are the services Sarah's clients received.

A Clients

- *Quarterly portfolio reviews, followed by any necessary rebalancing.* Because Sarah needed assets, she was talking with a broad range of prospects, some of whom weren't a perfect fit. But in her onboarding meetings, she made clear that she reviewed her investment portfolios monthly, and as soon as was most appropriate for her clients their investments would be allocated into the appropriate portfolios. Sarah had her clients complete her customized four-page risk assessment questionnaire and used that to assess which of her models best suited particular clients' risk tolerances and investment goals. (If you need such a questionnaire for yourself, Morningstar offers one that has been popular among advisors.) She was determined to stick to this approach from the start so she didn't create an unwieldy investment management issue for herself; she had heard her colleague Ron down the hall complaining about that.

- *Annual insurance reviews.* Sarah believed and told her new clients that reviewing their insurance details was an important part of sound financial planning. However, she also recognized she didn't yet have the depth of expertise in this field, and so she turned to her colleague Robert who had his insurance license and had advised many clients about insurance details. He was happy to work with Sarah to assess various policies and even sit in on the occasional meeting with her. She trusted him to point out relevant details and educate her about how she could possibly help her clients be prepared for the unexpected, such as for disability or other significant health events. If she hadn't found Robert internally, she would have found a highly regarded, local insurance provider to build a relationship with and be one of her team (as long as this was agreeable with her firm or office manager).

- *Annual 401(k) reviews.* Sarah quickly established herself as a thoughtful advisor by asking for clients' latest 401(k) statements to gain an accurate, holistic picture of their investments. She explained she wanted to ensure they were not doubling up on identical asset classes in their 401(k)s and in their investments with her. She also told clients she wanted to safeguard against taking on inappropriate levels of risk, given their stated risk tolerance and investment objectives. She clarified that while she didn't have any direct access to their 401(k) portfolio, she was happy to review it for them and advise accordingly.

- *Tax return reviews.* Sarah stressed she was not a tax professional and did not provide tax advice. However, she did ask to see clients' latest tax returns and made electronic copies of them so she knew exactly what her clients earned, if they had carryforward losses that she could use to begin repositioning their investments, and what their tax bracket was. This also helped her gain greater insight into clients' personal balance sheets and cash flow circumstances, which allowed her to develop a more complete picture of their financial situations. By advising with a holistic approach, Sarah began distinguishing herself from other advisors who were more narrowly focused on clients' investment portfolios. Sarah also requested the names of her clients' CPAs, along with permission to talk to them should she need to discuss questions related to their tax returns or financial situations. She introduced herself to the CPAs and determined if they might be people with whom she wanted to build her referral network.

Sarah offered her A clients face-to-face quarterly reviews, and before each meeting was over she penciled a date in her calendar for their next meeting three months later. She told them she would contact them when their next review was approaching to confirm the appointment. Immediately after the meeting Sarah entered notes and reminders from that meeting into her client relationship management (CRM) system (for example, Act!, Redtail, or Salesforce). She then sent her clients a written summary of the meeting, made any necessary changes to their portfolios, and followed up on anything else.

While Sarah would be available to her A clients for four face-to-face meetings, she also wanted to ascertain individual clients' expectations. As they built trust after a couple of meetings, some clients preferred to meet only twice a year. With her narrow yet complete selection of investment options, clients saw that she had conviction for her process and stuck to her rationale. They got comfortable hearing similar feedback about their situation from Sarah at each meeting and gained confidence that she was attentively and effectively managing their portfolios. Because of this, they did not feel a need to directly connect with her more frequently.

Sarah also offered to do phone reviews, which were more convenient than regular face-to-face meetings for many of her clients. If the reviews did take place over the phone, she used a secure email system to send clients pertinent quarterly statements or had them access information through her online broker-dealer portal so they could see the same information she was seeing and referring to during the review. Meeting less frequently and over the phone was fine with Sarah. She still offered great, attentive service that kept her clients happy, but such adjustments also freed more of her time to continue building her business and servicing other clients.

B Clients

Sarah's B clients received the same degree of professionalism, just not as often. She provided them a portfolio review three times a year (every four months), with two face-to-face meetings and one phone meeting. At

WHAT TO INCLUDE IN YOUR MIX

While definitely not an exhaustive list, some services you might want to consider when deciding what to include in your own mix are:

- Personal balance sheet update

- Financial plan and subsequent updates

- Investment portfolio review

- Education planning

- 401(k) review

- Social Security analysis

- Insurance review (life, disability, liability, long-term care, key person, etc.)

- Estate plan review

- Gifting initiatives

- Wealth transition strategies

- Online access to accounts

any particular meeting, if clients indicated they would like to meet with Sarah again sooner than four months, she let them know that she valued their peace of mind but was comfortable with how their present situation was looking. Then she would immediately schedule their next meeting in four months so they would know exactly when they would connect with Sarah again, which greatly helped put their minds at ease. She emphasized that she was keeping an eye on their portfolio and gently but firmly clarified to those clients that three reviews a year were absolutely sufficient for how they were financially situated.

As she did with her A clients, Sarah requested their updated insurance information, latest 401(k) statements, most recent tax returns, and CPA details. Sarah also asked both her A and B clients for referrals using the approach discussed in Chapter 5.

C Clients

Sarah offered her C clients two portfolio reviews a year, with one face-to-face meeting and one phone call, covering the same information and providing the same high-quality service as with her A and B clients. Again, she requested updated insurance details, tax information, 401(k) statements, and CPA contact information.

D Clients

Sarah's D clients received two phone call reviews each year. Some of her service levels shifted a little as her business grew. As she needed to move C clients to D level, she encouraged more phone meetings and staggered call cycles so that over time she continued freeing more of her time for new, larger clients. She actively managed client expectations and stuck to her process, remaining focused on finding her ideal clients and building a great business.

Inherited Clients

After being in production for several months, Sarah's office manager was impressed with her focus and how she was structuring her business. There was a retiring advisor in the office who wanted to separate his lowest level clients from his book before handing it over to a partner. The manager decided to give Sarah those lower-level accounts. Sarah knew that the firm considered these to be effectively "dead assets" (accounts with small balances that people typically think aren't worth much time to pursue), and she assumed most of these people would end up in her D group of clients, but she decided to make the best of the opportunity. She asked Bill, the retiring advisor, to introduce her to these clients via email. Bill agreed and also decided to contact a few of them by phone to tell them of upcoming changes and mention they would be hearing from Sarah.

Sarah then contacted these people by email to introduce herself and offer some dates and times for a phone call to talk with them further and get to know their goals and investment objectives. She let them know that Bill had told her a little about them and that she was looking forward to the opportunity to meet them and see if working together would be a good fit. She did not assume they would want to work with her, and she also wanted to ensure that they would be a good match for the type of business she intended to build.

STAGE TWO: TWO TO FIVE YEARS

Ben was a "stage two" advisor. When he completed his training three years earlier, his manager had a couple of larger producers transition some of their lower-level clients to Ben, thinking this would help him get a good start and gain some momentum in building his business. When some advisors left Ben's office to work elsewhere or retire, he inherited some of their clients. Over time, Ben also brought on various clients himself. While his business grew, he was not discerning about managing clients' expectations. He permitted anyone to come aboard with him and did not have a system to organize them efficiently. Understandably, he was more focused on answering their questions about their investments rather than developing his own investment rationale to communicate to them. He didn't allocate time to develop a process to manage his business, and by year three Ben felt swamped.

When he looked at his book, he realized he had a hodge-podge of clients, along with their various investments and widely differing expectations of him. Every client phone call brought a different issue, specific to just that particular client. His portfolio reviews had no underlying, repeatable structure or format. His clients owned lots of different mutual funds, had many individual stocks, and often wanted to talk about market performance and "the next big thing." This was a far cry from how Ben wanted his clients to see him: a trusted, key financial advisor, overseeing their financial well-being and helping them with vital decisions throughout their lives.

Ben remembered his initial vision of the business he wanted to build, but he saw he was a long way from that picture. More frustrating was the feeling that vision was drifting further away with each new less-than-ideal referral he received and permitted aboard. He was frustrated. Instead of planning for growth with new clients and effectively servicing and helping existing ones, he felt stuck in reaction mode, constantly putting out client fires and scrambling to stay on top of everything. He inwardly shrank from bringing on new clients because he felt like he was just bringing on new headaches.

Ben began focusing on taking small but effective steps. He saw that he definitely had the ability to build a thriving business. What he needed most was a clear example of how to restructure things.

Because his clients held such a diverse mix of investments, Ben first ranked his clients by AUM so he could objectively see what assets he had.

And with no underlying, consistent investment structure, he also lacked an underpinning, unifying fee structure. So, to see what income was coming from where, he then ranked his clients by revenue. He needed to objectively know who his most valuable clients were before he could begin communicating that some things were about to change.

Once he had a handle on which clients were responsible for what revenue, he made necessary adjustments to his master list of client rankings to split his book into four levels, A to D. In his initial grouping, Ben's top 22 clients made up his A group. His B group consisted of 44 clients, the C group held 54 clients, and the D group had 26 clients. But his list was still a work in progress. Ben considered moving a number of his top B clients, who were among some of his favorites to work with and had potential for future asset growth, to his A group. After weighing this, though, he realized that would create distractions and would not leave much room for growth in the area where he most wanted it. Finally, Ben decided not to worry about where his favorite clients were going to end up in the mix, and he pushed his lowest 10 A clients into his B group to give himself more capacity to focus on hunting for more of his most desirable clients.

Ben began systematically implementing client reviews, focusing on in-person meetings for his A clients so he could talk directly with them and clarify that because his business had grown significantly over several years he needed to restructure. He told clients that he was beginning to limit the range of investments he would watch because more and more of his clients were looking to him for advice regarding important life issues. For this reason, he wanted to focus more on those areas rather than just adding another voice to the plentiful market commentary already available about individual stocks. He explained that he was developing a portfolio of more limited, yet effective investment offerings that would cater to his clients' needs. He assured clients that the transition of their investments to the new portfolio would happen carefully, but confirmed that was where he was headed with his business. He told A clients that most times he would meet with them quarterly to conduct a portfolio review, either in-person or, if they preferred, over the phone. He found almost all of his clients were just fine with the new schedule.

He implemented the same elements and frequency for reviews as Sarah did for her client tiers. He loved the feeling of gaining some control again and found that for the first time in quite a while he could proactively consider some marketing initiatives to help him grow his business. What struck Ben most in this restructuring process was how much time he had been spending on his D clients, with small balances and little loyalty, yet constant, time-consuming questions.

Initially some clients sounded a little skeptical about how Ben's changes were going to work. However, once they met with him and saw the process in action for several months, they appreciated Ben's longer-term focus and the perspective he took toward their major financial concerns. He educated his clients about what they really needed to be aware of for their financial health, rather than allowing them to get caught up in daily market fluctuations. They quickly realized the depth of Ben's advice and experience, and higher quality referrals started coming in.

There were some clients who wanted to continue plying Ben with questions about the latest start-ups, but he consistently and gently explained that while he enjoyed working with them and helping them, there was only so much value he could bring if they wanted to chase the latest market gyrations. A few clients weren't interested in the change, and so he suggested taking their accounts to online brokers like Scottrade, E*Trade, or TD Ameritrade that could be a better fit. He explained to those clients that they would have great access to a range of stock information, learn more about how markets work, and trade more cheaply than they could do with him. And he offered to send them the appropriate transfer paperwork to make that change simple for them. (We'll cover letting go of clients in Chapter 7.) A few clients moved their accounts, but Ben knew that losing those assets was only temporary. He quickly gained new clients who appreciated what he was offering and were willing to work together in the way he had restructured his business. Ben was polite, helpful, yet firm, and his clients knew where he stood and what he offered. He developed conviction for his process and began enjoying figuring out how to get in front of more A-level prospects.

STAGE THREE: VETERAN ADVISORS

Ron and his partner Steve had been in business together for 10 years. They had what appeared to be a successful practice, but they were at capacity. They kept taking on new clients, mostly referrals by the time I met them, but they felt frazzled. Like Ben, they had accepted new clients and their different investments without adhering to a sound, consistent investment process. They didn't realize when they started that while their asset levels quickly grew, they would eventually be faced with the tough task of needing to restructure. Over the years they had met and spoken about following a set asset-based fee schedule, but they had often relented and offered discounts when they learned prospects were seeking pricing information from other advisors in the area.

When they began, they claimed they wanted to focus on providing great financial advice for their clients and their clients' families. They had initially intended to use a number of good third-party money managers, but instead decided they liked the idea of providing a more personal, customized touch to managing their clients' investment holdings. Steve particularly liked monitoring and picking individual investments for clients, so at first it didn't seem to be a great inconvenience.

They also prided themselves on being highly accessible to their clients. When they first mentioned how often some of their clients contacted them—sometimes two to three times a week—they were proud of the close and trusting relationships they had developed with many of them. However, as they more closely analyzed where their time was being spent, they began to see these frequent phone calls more as signs of dependency than trust—a dependency that they had permitted to develop and even cultivated. They realized making themselves so available was one of the factors hampering them from following through with their various business development ideas.

Ron and Steve both knew what they needed to do, but old habits and busy schedules made making changes slow and challenging. To turn their situation around, they started with segmenting their book, then defining service models for their four groups and fully and consistently following these with no exceptions. They knew instinctively they needed to go back a couple of steps, slow down their growth, and build a scalable business system that was manageable and would allow their clients to benefit from their years of experience and significant industry knowledge. Talking about changing how they did things was simple; however, they knew that making changes required a clear vision and adjusting their business structure and daily practices.

Analyze Where the Money Comes From

First, Ron and Steve looked at exactly how their business was operating financially. Because they had permitted their book to grow without consistent direction, clients were being charged a range of different fees. Some were receiving discounts based on "house-holding" assets (charging a smaller fee per account based on the aggregated balance that a family holds), but that wasn't overly difficult to navigate. The tougher fee-related issue was that they had allowed clients moving to them to dictate that they would pay no more than they had paid their previous advisor. Instead of pointing out that this was going to be a different relationship than the one they were leaving and emphasizing their specific investment rationale and holdings, Ron and Steve had relented and let new clients dictate their fees. The advisors did not clarify what they expected from relationships with their clients and what clients could expect from them at the outset.

I advised them to first focus on client rankings by revenue so they could see who they were deriving their income from and effectively decide how to position those clients into their new various asset models. Then they correlated that information with their client rankings by AUM and saw that some of their clients with the largest assets were actually not the most profitable. They had a sense this was perhaps the case before formally doing this exercise, but seeing the real revenue rankings in writing was a great motivator to persevere in making the changes they wanted and not slipping back into old limiting habits.

Stick to a Uniform Fee Structure

Ron and Steve determined to stop their habit of capitulating on fees to attract new clients. Instead, when faced with prospects who were reluctant to accept a higher fee, they clarified that prospects were looking to leave their previous advisors because they were unhappy. They did some research into what firms in their area were charging advisory clients, and even with their higher fees they believed they charged a fair price for great personal service and advice and were ready to tell prospects why they did not discount their fees.

Create A to D Groups

From there, they created A to D groups based on clear information about which clients provided them the greatest to the least value. The placements were a combination of objective and subjective factors; they considered revenue generated and asset levels, as well as how agreeable particular clients were to work with and their receptivity to the advisors' advice. Even though some clients didn't fit neatly into one specific group, Ron and Steve agreed not to procrastinate and proceeded to complete this project within a month, knowing that if they felt it was wise they could make changes as they implemented their new structure. Going forward, the frequency of their contacts with clients would be determined by their group placements. All clients (A through D) would receive the same levels of high-quality service and care, but A clients would receive more attention and interaction from Ron and Steve than D clients.

Manage Client Expectations with a Planned Service Structure

Initially Ron and Steve were concerned about what clients would think when they told them about upcoming changes, but they quickly realized they could simply begin adjusting some call cycles without clients feeling any major changes. To keep on track, they kept reminding themselves that the reason for undertaking this project was to ultimately free more time to bring on new clients and alleviate pressure from randomly servicing existing ones. They did clarify for some clients who were used to having access multiple times each week that constant reviews of their portfolio holdings were just not necessary. They explained they were continually watching *all* their clients' investments from a big-picture perspective and that being too reactionary was a sure-fire way of making decisions based on emotions rather than reason. They pointed out they did not do this, nor did they recommend their clients approach managing their money this way. Ron and Steve reiterated they were restructuring their business and schedules to allocate more strategic and focused attention to their overall investment philosophy and process.

Reduce Investment Choices

Both partners realized that by claiming to take fiduciary responsibility for clients' accounts and be trusted advisors, they needed to be able to maintain a deep level of knowledge about all of the investments in their book, have clear opinions about those investments, and clearly communicate the reason behind having their clients hold particular positions. They accepted that to be able to do this meant significantly reducing their investment offerings. Instead of holding 55 mutual funds all covering the same market sector, they agreed to review various fund managers and decide on their own rationale for selecting a single fund or third-party manager to cover a particular sector. Then they could begin considering the implications of moving individual clients into those funds. The process took time, but like Ben, they began informing existing clients that the high level of service and detailed attention they were used to receiving would continue as the firm standardized its investment offerings. Ron and Steve clarified that as markets moved and it was advantageous to do so, they would begin reallocating clients' holdings to be in line with their closely monitored models.

GETTING STARTED

Segmenting your book into different service tiers and creating a limited choice of investment models are foundational keys to creating a scalable, manageable business. If you've heard about segmenting your book but keep putting it off, now is the time to stop making excuses and take action. Assembling your tiers is not a perfect science, and it will require both focus and some subjective considerations, but there are some guidelines you may find helpful in applying the process to your book.

Begin by classifying your clients by AUM. Place the top 10 percent of clients in your A group. (If you have 120 clients, you'll have 12 in this tier.) Sometimes you'll have reasons why you think a particular client would be better in the B group than the A group, but don't be concerned about subjective considerations yet. Place your next 20 percent of clients into your B group (24 clients in our example). Forty percent of your clients will go into your C group (48 clients), and the remaining 30 percent (36 clients) will make up your D group. By initially weighting your C and D groups, you will allow room for growth in your A and B groups. To effectively grow a more profitable business, you will not want to take on any more C or D clients; the growth you desire will come primarily from adding more clients that match the criteria for your A clients.

Once these initial divisions are made, decide how you will service the people in your various tiers. Can you effectively service these clients as often as you would like?

- If you want to hold quarterly review meetings with your A clients, does that seem realistic with the number of A clients you have? For instance, with 12 A clients, you would need to hold a review meeting with four of them each month so that you could see each of them four times per year.

- If you want to meet with your 24 B clients three times a year, split over two face-to-face meetings and one phone call review, you will need to schedule meetings with these clients once every four months. This translates to six meetings with clients from this group each month. With this group, you have the time-saving benefit of one phone meeting each year. (Remember, you can email the details you'll be discussing, provided you have a secure system in place for doing this, or mail the material if you have a client who isn't tech savvy.)

- If you want to meet your 48 C clients twice each year, once face-to-face and once by phone, you will need to average eight meetings per month with these clients.

- To have a review with your 36 D clients twice a year by phone, you will need to schedule six of these calls per month.

All up, you would be looking to have 24 meetings, either in person or by phone, each month—that's six each week, or more than one per day. Does that seem reasonable to you? If not, something will need fine-tuning: either the dividing points for some of your groupings need to change or you need to adjust your service model. Another option could be to decide to bring on a junior advisor to help service your lower-tier clients, but this would be a part of a larger business strategy decision. At this stage, just focus on how many meetings you need to have each week and whether that sounds manageable to you. You can see how this process allows you to plan your schedule to gain a sense of the reality of the time requirements to run your business.

Even after this process, your groupings aren't set in stone. Are there people who you know have considerable assets held outside your firm that you feel you are close to getting? If so, and they're currently B clients and you have some capacity in your scheduling, maybe you want to elevate them to A clients. Or, maybe you want to assign them a different designation, such as A*. Just be judicious in this process: make sure there is a good reason, other than the fact that you simply find them fun people to work with, before moving people to a higher tier.

Once you have created a framework with these first divisions, fine-tune your groups so you are comfortable that the right clients are in the correct groups. Even if the bottom couple of clients in your A tier don't have many more assets or generate much more revenue than your top B clients, don't elevate your B clients. Remember that your clients don't know how they've been ranked, so they're not going to feel slighted. And you're not going to slight them; you simply must have a way of tracking your clients to ensure that you deliver the most effective service possible to keep them happy, grow your business, and maintain your sanity and health.

Placements will change over time. Perhaps a C client inherits assets that rank them in the middle of your A group. You don't need to announce that you are changing their servicing tier; simply begin scheduling their reviews a little more frequently. Of course, any changes or additions will change your capacity and may affect how you maintain a reasonable schedule.

The process might take you several days, or even several weeks, but it is essential that you commit to it! Analyze where your income is coming from and then create appropriate groups where servicing them is relatively easy to monitor. As I said, it's not an exact science with hard and fast percentages or strict division lines. Even advisors with books that look identical on paper are likely to end up with slightly different groupings based on personalities and business goals. However, you must begin somewhere if your goal is to maintain (or regain) control of your business. By taking this step honestly, you'll begin to build your process and better manage existing clients while being able to devote time to business-building and administrative activities.

Advisors I work with usually aren't surprised when I ask them to segment their books in this way; there's been plenty written in our industry about doing this. However, it can be a real challenge to do because it takes time and deliberate effort. A benefit in working with a coach who has experience in this business is that you have someone to bounce ideas off of and who knows what works, as well as stumbling blocks you may face. A coach will also hold you accountable to avoid distraction and procrastination and finally get it done if you keep putting it off.

Once advisors follow through and complete this task, they come back excited, refreshed, and full of great ideas because suddenly their business feels a lot more manageable. Many say it makes them feel like they can get their arms around their business, some for the first time, even after being in business for several years. Advisors begin seeing more clearly how to grow in manageable and quantifiable ways and are more focused on doing that. They know exactly what their A clients look like, how those people behave, and how many they have. After doing this, often the first thing advisors want to discuss in their next coaching session is how they can find more of those A clients. Some see the need to bring on an assistant or junior advisor, and because they have reviewed their revenue and profitability they can see where and how to generate the additional revenue to effectively cover that new overhead. This step allows you to get realistic about your objectives and specific about the steps required to achieve them so you can start making noticeable progress toward your goals.

Once you have your client tiers and meeting frequency in place, begin to build a list of specific deliverables and a way to track them. These will be the key services you'll provide to your clients at the designated times. Each client touch will be programmed into your schedule and tracked so you'll know what's coming and what's been done. Use your CRM system to input details clearly and add follow-up communication to your calendar. This will ensure you don't have your best ideas on yellow pads or miscellaneous scattered sheets of paper that can be easily misplaced and clutter both your desk and your mind. If you have an assistant or partner who also has direct contact with your clients, precise notes will be invaluable to their being able to provide top-level service, even in your absence. With good records and calendaring, you won't have to worry because you'll have a system to ensure your clients are being taken care of. This will also allow you to see when you can focus on other crucial activities that bring in new clients and uncover fresh assets.

Decide what items are important for your clientele and then determine what you will cover with clients and when. Not every item will be covered at every meeting. Each meeting (whether quarterly, every four months, or semiannual) will include a portfolio review, but other issues can be addressed over time. If you have not already gathered in-depth financial information to prepare a financial plan, at your first meeting you may request to see a client's latest tax return.

If you plan to cover insurance and estate planning issues at your second meeting, mention this at the first meeting. Then, let your clients know you will send them details regarding the documents you'd like to see before their next meeting, so you can be prepared to discuss their situation as it relates to these issues. Midyear meetings are a great time to bring up year-end gifting and communicate the benefits and intricacies of that with relevant clients. For clients approaching age 62, you'll want to address Social Security issues, helping them understand their options and maybe even calling the Social Security Administration with them on the line to make sure everything is clear. Plan your review meetings so you and your clients know you are thoroughly considering and monitoring their financial well-being. Of course, you will follow up any verbal requests made during the meeting with reminders for your clients in emailed meeting summaries. If you need documents before your next meeting, communicate that you will send them a written checklist with a return envelope to get everything back to you (and then calendar a time to do that).

DISTRACTION-PROOF STEPS

1. Segment your book into A, B, C, and D clients.

2. Determine appropriate services and their frequency for each group.

3. Keep clear notes and a detailed calendar.

Segmenting your book of clients gives you a better view of your business and allows you to control and manage client interactions. You can more effectively prioritize your time and focus, giving you greater control over the services you provide your clients. The structure will ensure you are looking after all your clients thoroughly and put you in a better position to receive more referrals from your happy A clients.

Sometimes, however, you will have clients who call you their advisor but consistently refuse or second-guess your advice. These clients can end up taking a lot of your time and emotional energy. In the next chapter, we'll cover some ways to manage client expectations and what to do with clients who no longer fit into your business model.

CHAPTER SEVEN
AVOID DETOURS

*"Our goals can only be reached through a vehicle of a plan,
in which we must fervently believe, and upon which we must
vigorously act. There is no other route to success."*

– PABLO PICASSO, ARTIST AND COFOUNDER OF CUBISM

Tolerating behavior from clients that is contrary to your underlying business philosophy will pull you off track. You'll be distracted by:

- Trying to accommodate people who don't fit your business structure

- Spending time with clients who don't value your advice, often at the expense of clients who do

- Fatigue from spreading yourself too thinly

Change can be tough. While it's often pleasant to contemplate results that change might produce, actually implementing systemic change takes focus, time, and perseverance. If you need to streamline your business and communicate with clients how you'll be working going forward, you need to be committed to the change—this means acting deliberately and anticipating the extra effort required (even if the effort is short term). Initially, establishing definite criteria for whom you want as clients, what your range of investment offerings will be, and how you will operate your system for servicing clients may feel uncomfortably limiting or intimidating, especially if it means making major changes in the way you have been doing business. Some clients may not be happy with the changes you want to make. However, establishing these procedures makes running your business more manageable, expandable, and fun. When you continuously focus on longer-term objectives, each day can move you closer to your ideal business working with your ideal clients. In this chapter, we'll look at how to navigate potential roadblocks when trying to change how you operate your business.

I grew up in New Zealand, where I began swimming at the age of 8. While I couldn't even swim one length of the pool when I started, things soon changed. By the age of 14, I was winning national titles and began competing internationally. By the time I was enrolled at the University of California at Berkeley at age 18, I had years of national titles, international age-group titles, and world rankings under my belt. I had developed my swimming style, and from what I and others could see, it seemed to be working. However, my new college coach could see I had developed a pattern in my stroke that would limit how far I could go. He knew if I kept up the same technique I would never get much faster, and I'd likely blow my elbow sooner or later. He insisted I change my stroke. It was different from how I had done it for my whole career. When I swam this new way, I felt weak and uncomfortable, and it made me slower. Even though races against my teammates were inconsequential in the long term, it irked me that this new stroke was making me lose to guys much less experienced than I was. More than once I wanted to give up and go back to doing things the way I had always done them. I felt that while it may not have been ideal, it hadn't really been that bad, and most of all it was familiar and comfortable. But, my coach knew that for me to reach my goal of being among the very top swimmers in the world, I had to endure this short-term discomfort for long-term gain.

If you have an established business, what changes do you need to make to the way you do business in order to realize your goals sooner? What activities or procedures do you avoid because it seems like it's just too much effort? If you have been following the process in this book, most of the changes you will have made to your business approach so far likely have not been too difficult. Fitting new clients into investment models is not problematic, especially when your approach and rationale are clearly presented from the time of your first exploratory meeting together. Even turning away prospects who aren't a good fit probably has not been too awkward because you never had their assets in your fold to start with and knew you were saving yourself future headaches. But what about making changes with existing clients—the ones you have known for years? Maybe some of your working relationships aren't ideal, taking up more of your time than you'd like, but you're familiar with them and know what they want from you. You may not be eager to implement changes with them because you're worried about how they may respond. If you're seeing positive results from other changes, it may be even easier to come up with excuses why you don't address issues with existing clients. After all, you may think that as long as you are making positive changes in your business, why rock the boat. But to get the business you really want, you may need to streamline the way you work with both new and existing clients. The short-term inconvenience involved in operating in new ways may not immediately feel great—initially it may even seem like more work—but it is worth the long-term benefits.

ANTICIPATING OUTCOMES

Elizabeth and Diane were advisory partners in a similar situation to Ron and Steve in the previous chapter. Elizabeth had been an advisor for 16 years, and she and Diane had been partners for 11 years. They had a nice business; they were not the largest producers in their region, but they had good client relationships and made comfortable incomes. Their clients liked them, and their business growth came mostly from referrals. While they appreciated the friends and family clients sent their way, they felt inundated by any new business because their systems were inconsistent. For the past couple of years, Elizabeth had toyed with the idea of only working four days a week. Every so often she would try it for a couple of weeks, but always ended up feeling more stressed because there was always so much to do. They knew they had the potential to have an outstanding business, but they also realized they weren't going to get there the way they had been going.

So, they talked about ways to change things. They discussed ideas they had read about in trade publications. Elizabeth even subscribed to a coaching service for advisors and shared what she heard on phone calls and webinars with Diane. They often reviewed their fees and conferred about raising them. They deliberated about restructuring and considered how they would begin. They talked at length about what fund managers to cull, but regularly justified leaving clients' investments just as they were, often for sentimental reasons. They talked about making major changes in their business after this quarter was completed. They kept talking and talking and talking. They had been talking for years, but it just never seemed to be the right time to make definitive and permanent changes. It felt too uncomfortable to slow down and do things in a new way, although they intellectually understood the benefits of doing so. It just felt easier to stay with what was familiar.

When I first asked them to segment their book into A, B, C, and D clients, they resisted. Elizabeth said she knew a lot of industry coaches said best practices meant firing the bottom quarter to half of your book, or at least relegating them to a call center. She said that she understood that getting rid of these clients might streamline their business, but she just wasn't going to do that. She was quick to defend their smaller clients, explaining that many of them had been her first clients when she was getting started as an advisor and had been with her more than 15 years. They had trusted her and been loyal all these years, and that meant a lot to her. She felt particularly protective of several elderly clients who had been friends of her parents when they were still alive. Elizabeth knew they wouldn't be particularly attractive clients for other advisors, and she said she didn't feel it was right to just set them adrift.

She was surprised when I agreed with her. I affirmed that those clients had believed in her and stuck with her while she was learning and finding her way as an advisor. I understood that she got into advising not only because she wanted to build her own business, but also because she genuinely cared about people and wanted to help them. I told her I understood her sense of protectiveness and loyalty to these people who had been loyal to her, and I definitely did not recommend firing them just because they had small asset balances. What she needed to do was move their investments into the appropriate model portfolios, which would make monitoring their holdings efficient. We discussed that, of course, she would be careful to consider any applicable tax implications, and movements of assets would be done with market fluctuations in mind.

Elizabeth was still hesitant to suggest changes to their clients, but she proceeded with preparing the emails to the D clients, advising them of the changes she and Diane had finally committed to make and requesting a time to talk about details. Here's a sample of what she wrote:

Hi Joe and Helen,

I hope you had a fun weekend. I trust you're both well and wanted to see if we could schedule a brief phone call sometime next week, please.

With business continuing to grow, Diane and I are implementing some changes to allow us to continue to help clients who, like you, are serious about their financial futures. We are reducing the quantity of investment choices we are monitoring and encouraging clients to move their assets into carefully chosen and watched investment models we have established. (This change will not affect the fees applicable to your accounts.) While these changes will allow us to closely monitor our investment holdings, more importantly they will ensure we have even more time to maintain high-quality focus on clients' larger key financial issues like planning, retirement, Social Security details, and other big-picture concerns.

Knowing your needs and objectives, I'd like to review your current holdings with you and explain what next steps might look like in making adjustments to these. Do you have about 45 minutes for a phone call next week, possibly sometime between

12 pm and 2 pm, on Tuesday, May 15th, please, so we can discuss potential changes to your accounts?

Thanks Joe, thanks Helen. I'm looking forward to speaking with you both.

Elizabeth and Diane had thought the process of making the investment changes would be difficult. They worried that clients were simply going to say no to moving into their new model portfolios, but instead they were pleased to find most clients were accepting. Once they explained the rationale for recommending the new investments to their clients and outlined how these changes fit their investment objectives, most clients were fine making their recommended changes. Clients' most common concern was whether or not their fees were going to increase. Although their original email addressed this, Elizabeth and Diane reemphasized that their fee structure would stay the same and clarified that the changes would mean they could keep an even closer eye on clients' investments, for the same fee.

Over and over again clients reaffirmed their trust in Elizabeth and Diane's ability and professionalism. While the specific comments varied from client to client, the theme remained consistent: "You're the professionals and the ones watching what's going on. I don't want to have to watch things every day, and that's why I pay you. I trust you to make recommendations that make sense for where we want to go." Having clients express confidence in and appreciation for the services they provided made Elizabeth and Diane feel good. These clients understood they would continue having twice-yearly phone appointments to review their investments and overall financial situation.

Their D clients remained less profitable than their A clients, but because their investments fit into their models, the partners could serve these clients effectively and efficiently. Also, Elizabeth was thinking about retiring in a few years, and their sales assistant, Jessie, had expressed interest in eventually becoming an advisor. Elizabeth and Diane had already discussed beginning to bring Jessie in on some meetings and quickly recognized that having her start interacting with their D clients could be an ideal place for her to start learning the advisory side of the business. Jessie would be able to spend a little more time with these clients and possibly uncover fresh assets. Most important, she would learn new skills that would later help her assist Diane with larger clients when Elizabeth started stepping back from the day-to-day business operations.

Elizabeth and Diane focused on reallocating investments in the accounts of their smallest clients and those with the least tax-sensitive retirement accounts first. Once they had done this, they were even more comfortable with and committed to their investment portfolios. They were both eager to continue streamlining their book, working their way through their remaining clients. Diane saw how it would create a lot more capacity to take on new clients in a manageable way, which would be good for the long-term health of the business. Going forward, as soon as was prudent given potential tax consequences and trading costs, most new clients' investments were adjusted to fit into one of the model portfolios based on their personal risk tolerance and financial objectives. If that didn't interest them, both Elizabeth and Diane were fine to let them go, because they knew those prospects didn't fit their way of doing business. The process to move their existing clients' assets into their investment models took almost a year, but as they kept seeing the positive changes the restructuring brought to their business and their own schedules, they became more and more committed to continuing the process of making the changes.

There were a few larger clients who had investments outside of their portfolio models that made sense to hold onto: stocks with an extremely low cost basis in taxable accounts, incentive stock options, and even stocks with sentimental value. (One older client had stock her father had given her that paid good dividends, and Elizabeth knew it would be heartbreaking to her client to sell these stocks, no matter how rational it might be.) In each case Elizabeth and Diane clearly explained to clients that they would not be regularly monitoring the performance of those stocks, and they confirmed this in letters to those clients.

Typically twice a year, in preparation for review meetings, the advisors would pull reports for the stocks a client held outside of their models to determine if it might be a good time to consider selling those equities and reallocating the funds into their models. Elizabeth and Diane used reports from their firm's internal stock analysts for this, but other reports, such as those available from Value Line, Standard & Poor's, or Morningstar, provide similar information. They firmly set their rationale for determining whether to recommend selling particular equities, based on ratings from the reports they used, and clearly explained this to clients during their reviews. If clients agreed to sell at that time, the advisors made the transactions. If clients preferred to hold on to what they had, Elizabeth and Diane reiterated that they would look at the equities again in about six months and make appropriate recommendations then. In the meantime they reminded clients that they would not be monitoring the performance of those equities because they were outside of their recommended portfolios.

HOW TO SEPARATE YOURSELF FROM CLIENTS WHO DON'T FIT YOUR BUSINESS

Another advisor, John, also committed to changing how he had been doing business. When we first started our coaching relationship he told me he always felt very productive when he was researching companies his clients held, especially when he did this for new clients and was able to share information they were not aware of. After ranking his clients, though, he saw he was spending too much time doing this, and probably not enough time interacting with some of his larger clients. While some of his midsized clients were recommending him to their friends, he identified a few clients (both large and small) who were always contacting him with their market perspectives and opinions. When he thought about it, he admitted that these clients never really listened to his advice regarding their longer-term investment objectives, even though they had initially voiced such plans at their first meeting.

Ryan was one of John's more transaction-oriented clients, and he particularly enjoyed closely following the financial markets. John knew he needed to tell Ryan he wasn't going to be watching the daily details of equities like he once did and instead would focus on specific groups of investments in his model portfolios. John had already spoken to a number of his clients and knew that this new approach suited most of them, but it didn't appeal to everyone. After he processed some initial pushback he got from clients, he felt okay that not all of his existing clients would agree to the changes he was making—he knew these changes suited him and were the most effective way for him to build his business the way he wanted to and reach his objectives. When Ryan next called, John explained the situation. He tried to help Ryan see that by tracking a smaller number of investments, he'd have more time to help clients plan more effectively for their future.

John thought carefully about how to say this to Ryan, practiced how to tactfully pose the situation in a context that would be easy for Ryan to relate to, and relayed to me what he planned to say. Ryan was an optometrist, and John thought drawing on this would be a good way to shape his point. Ryan had developed a specific area of expertise in his business, and John wanted to use this similarity to explain what he was doing in his advisory business.

"Think about your optometry practice," John said. "You focus on clients who have specific needs. While you could probably study and also help people with hearing issues, you've remained focused on helping people with issues and questions specifically regarding their vision. This is what I'm doing with my business—focusing on a specific process to help people with issues related to planning for their financial future. I enjoy working with you and would value continuing that. I think it'll be fun to watch how your business grows and see the different choices you'll have to make as you grow. I'd love to help you plan for some of those exciting situations. The changes I'm making in my investment process will allow me to be able to do that for you and other professionals I work with.

"If you want a couple of days to consider moving forward together, that's fine. I can call you next week to see what you've decided. Then we can take the next step of either changing your holdings, where appropriate, or I can help you with all the details of moving your account to another advisor who can be more available to discuss daily market activities and individual equities with you, or to an online account where you can manage your account yourself." John was polite and helpful, yet firm.

Ryan said he understood where John was coming from, and that he'd think about it. John let Ryan know again that he had enjoyed working with him, and that he would connect with him early the following week so Ryan could let him know what he wanted to do.

Immediately after John got off the phone, he wisely put all the details of his call with Ryan into his CRM system. He knew that situations like this could often become emotional, and he wanted everything to be clearly noted to help avoid any potential misunderstandings in the future.

STICK TO YOUR PLAN

Because newer advisors are still establishing their business processes and systems, they usually don't face the same challenges in relation to change the way more seasoned advisors do. Their main challenge comes in firmly setting a plan for their business structure and then patiently seeking and securing their ideal clients. When the pressure is on to bring in assets, *any* assets, to get a book established, it can be easy to veer off track, accepting people who aren't particularly receptive to your advice and just want someone to take orders from them, or take on someone for emotional reasons even though they aren't a good fit. Justifying excuses such as, "It's only one client," "I really need the assets," "We can make changes in their account later," "We'll get to know each other and it'll work out," come readily, but can quickly hamstring you.

The weekend after John explained his upcoming changes to Ryan, Ryan was at a local fundraising event where he met Sarah, the new advisor you read about in the last chapter. By this point she had been in production about eight months. They struck up a friendly conversation, and as Ryan told Sarah about his optometry practice and answered her questions about some of his future plans, Sarah quickly ascertained he had considerable money and great potential as a prospect. Sarah started getting excited when Ryan mentioned that he wasn't happy with his current advisor. He told Sarah that he wasn't getting his calls returned. Sarah became even more interested: she'd heard how advisors sometimes got too busy to manage all of their clients, even bigger ones, and that some clients grew so frustrated at not hearing back they looked for a new advisor.

Ryan expressed interest in possibly meeting with Sarah to discuss his investments. She suspected he could qualify as her first A client. Even though she felt excited, outwardly she remained calm. As she was handing him her card, she asked when he'd last heard from his advisor. He said he had finally talked to him the day before, but prior to then Ryan had been calling practically every day the previous week. He wanted to see if he should buy more Google stock or wait for a new IPO that he had been reading about, but he said his advisor just never got back to him. Sarah's heart sank because she definitely would have liked Ryan's assets but knew she didn't need a client with unreasonable demands.

Ryan carried on, excitedly telling her about the IPO, and started scrolling through his phone looking for details he wanted to read to her. Sarah took the opportunity to jump in and clarify again how she worked with her clients, focusing more on planning for longer-term outcomes and goals like retirement planning, children's education, and Social Security issues. She said Ryan kept making positive sounds, "uh-huhing" in response to what she said as he continued to scan his phone, but she sensed he really wasn't listening to what she was saying. While he focused on his phone and furiously kept scrolling, Sarah mentioned how she helped business owners and families work toward achieving their ideal financial landscape.

Ryan said his current advisor had been mentioning stuff like that. But, he told Sarah, there were sure a lot of great opportunities to make some serious quick money by paying attention to the markets each day, and he didn't want to lose out on that. Sarah politely responded that maybe this wasn't a good time for them to connect further since it sounded like his objectives were different from the types of goals she helped her clients with. She left the door open to help with any longer-term needs, such as the best retirement plans for self-employed business owners or selling his practice when he was ready to retire. While Sarah was disappointed that Ryan clearly wasn't a good fit, she was proud of herself for not letting her excitement get the best of her and for asking qualifying questions that helped her identify what he really wanted and that he was not a prospect she wanted to pursue. She moved on, continuing to focus on finding just the right prospects to round out her goal of bringing on 37 clients that year.

The following week, John got back in touch with Ryan, who had decided to move his account to an advisor who played tennis with his dad. John provided all the paperwork for Ryan to make an easy transition to his new advisor. John knew he had done right by Ryan and in relation to his own business. Ryan could move to another advisor or an online trading platform that suited his interests better, and John would stick to building his business with people he could help most.

MAKING EXCEPTIONS THAT MAKE SENSE

At the same event where Sarah met Ryan she also met Abby and Matthew, a young couple who had been married just a few years. Abby worked in biotech, and Matthew had just begun a career in IT security. Sarah spent a while talking with them and learning more about them and what they hoped for in their future. They were busy people, and they had been talking about starting to look for an advisor who understood them. They wanted someone they could trust and grow with over the long term. From what they told her, Sarah recognized they had good potential for asset growth and saw ways she could possibly help them. Both Abby and Matthew were clearly comfortable with her and were receptive to her explanation of her investment process and that she would be happy to talk with them further about financial planning.

Abby said she realized they didn't really have a lot of money at that stage, only a combined $85,000 in IRAs, and wondered if it was even worth working with an advisor. Sarah quickly noted to herself that Abby and Matthew's assets were below the minimum she had set for her business, and she really wanted to focus her prospecting on people with more assets who would fit in her A and B tiers. However, she really liked this couple. Prior to meeting Abby and Matthew, she had decided that if she met prospects who did not quite have the assets she was looking for but had strong potential for future asset growth and otherwise were a great fit, she would take them on if they agreed to pay her a minimum annual management fee of $1,750. This amount was equivalent to the 1.75 percent fee she charged her smallest clients who met her $100,000 asset minimum. In addition to being agreeable to the fee, they had to agree to follow her investment models and be responsive to her advice. Finally, she also required these clients to give her discretion over trading in their accounts. This approach ensured that prospects were serious and didn't waste Sarah's time. She would maximize the benefits of sticking to her limited investment platform because smaller clients could simply be integrated into her existing platform and would require little extra effort from her.

Sarah let Abby and Matthew know that while the amount of assets was one thing, having the right attitude to work together was even more important to her. She explained that she had met people who had a lot of money but were not necessarily a good fit for her to work with because they were more focused on chasing the latest hot stock than their long-term financial health. She clarified she chose not to do business with those folks. (Ryan was fresh on her mind!) She told them that if she met prospects who seemed to have a great attitude, even if they had a smaller account balance, she wouldn't guarantee taking them on as a client but was happy to meet and explore the possibility of working together. She said if everything else seemed like a great fit, she would charge a minimum fee for her services and advice, and then as their assets grew over time the fees for her services would transition to being based on decreasing percentages of their assets.

If you decide to set a minimum asset threshold for new clients, you'll have to make your own decision about how you'll handle both prospective and existing clients who have assets under that level. Minimum fees can give you flexibility to take on prospects with small assets but great potential, while ensuring you still get fairly compensated for your time and expertise. Younger prospects are often very amenable to the idea of paying a specific fee for set services, rather than only looking at fees as a percentage of their assets. If you have been in business a while and are refocusing on prospects with higher minimum assets, you will have to decide if those changes will impact your existing clients with smaller balances. Will you increase their fees to ensure you are being fairly compensated for the level of service you are providing? Of course, you would provide plenty of advance warning and a clear explanation of why you are doing so. Or, will you outline the changes you are making but clarify the new fees will only apply to new clients, so that those existing smaller clients see your business is thriving and appreciate the continued opportunity to work with you? If larger clients are interested in opening smaller accounts for children, you may want to mention you typically charge a minimum fee but offer the same household fee for immediate family members in order to keep assets with you.

There are many ways to work out the details. If you do consider making exceptions to your "rules," for both practical and fiduciary purposes you'll need to ensure you have consistent and compelling reasons beyond "they seem nice" that justify those exceptions. Your focus should always remain on looking for more A or B clients, with any additions to your Cs or Ds being exceptions. Keep your vision for your business in sight and choose actions that make sense in light of that vision.

When Sarah met with Abby and Matthew they agreed that having Sarah prepare a financial plan, which was separate from her investment advisory services, would be a good first step. This plan set an initial road map for where Abby and Matthew wanted to go. They saw how Sarah could help them on their journey, and they became part of her group of D clients. Sarah was careful in making her decision to take them on; she felt they were worth breaking her minimum asset rule because of their age, future potential, great attitude, and the good chemistry they seemed to have with her. She was clear about the contact they could expect from her and the services she would provide. While Sarah particularly enjoyed working with the couple, she did not count them toward her goal of 37 new clients for the year because they were below her minimum asset level. She remained focused on finding more clients with both the right attitude and the assets she had identified in her TARGET Goal.

FIRING CLIENTS

Occasionally you will have to fire a client. I don't recommend firing a large portion of your book just because they have small assets and are less profitable. Yes, you occasionally read about advisors who have done this and transformed their business, but this isn't realistic for most advisors I know. Ideally, this is a business based on relationships, and typically at least one of the major reasons people become advisors is that they want to help people. Firing clients just because they're small doesn't sit well with advisors who have adopted that helping approach, and we've covered how those smaller clients can be incorporated into your investment models and not take a lot of your time and effort.

However, I would encourage you not to hesitate to fire any client, small or large, who makes a habit of refusing to follow your investment process and who dismisses your advice or is repeatedly rude to your staff. Any client who consistently takes up disproportionate amounts of your valuable time and focus because they do not want to cooperate, despite your discussing these problems with them, should be let go—they do not respect your process and probably do not respect you. They are looking for something you do not offer (or no longer offer), and your business is the wrong place for them. If they walked into a Ford dealership and started telling the salesperson they were looking for a Toyota Prius, the salesperson might try to interest them in looking at a Ford Fusion. But if the person persisted, insisting that they wanted a Prius, despite the alternatives they were being offered, it would not take long for the Ford salesperson to direct them to the Toyota dealership and wish them a good day. If you have given resistant clients a choice between working within your business model or moving their accounts elsewhere, and they have chosen to stay but also resolutely want something you don't offer, it's time to stop the subtle suggestions that they would probably be happier elsewhere and be more direct.

If you are in this situation, proceed carefully. We're in a litigious culture and a very emotional industry. Be clear and objective about why working together with this particular person is no longer appropriate, and keep good notes at every step of the process. A sample of how you might end a relationship with a client who does not follow your advice might be the following:

> Our job is to provide advice and have clients follow that advice. When clients insist on handling their investments in ways that disregard our advice, we have to reevaluate the value we're adding to the relationship. That's the situation we're in with your account. We're concerned because we're not able to do our jobs fully. You seem to want services and an approach that we don't offer, and so we can't provide you with the value we want to give our clients. Working together is no longer a good fit, and we must insist you take your accounts elsewhere. There are some good online alternatives, and I'm sure you can find other people who will be happy to tell you their thoughts and recommendations.

If they need recommendations of where to take their accounts, provide some suggestions. Depending on your relationship with your broker-dealer or custodian, you may move their account to a help desk or delink their accounts. Keep your side of the conversation direct, professional, and unemotional: "Working together is no longer a good fit because.... We need to end our relationship with you and will be happy to provide you with suggestions about where you can take your account."

WHEN TO FIRE A CLIENT

Fire clients if:

- They are repeatedly rude to your staff.

- They do not follow your advice.

- They make unreasonable demands.

- They always complain.

- They refuse to respond to your repeated calls or emails.

- They won't adhere to your process.

Firing a client isn't fun. But you must take this step if someone is ignoring your advice and disrespecting the way you wish to operate your business. Don't delay in doing this. Take action and get them off your books so you no longer have fiduciary responsibility for their accounts. Don't let the issue grow into an even bigger problem. If you know you really need to get rid of a client, trust your instincts and take this difficult but productive step. Once you do, you'll likely tell yourself you really should have done it sooner. Then, refocus on your clients who trust, respect, and appreciate you and what you do for them.

DISTRACTION-PROOF STEPS

1. Don't assume clients will be resistant to moving into your portfolios or altering the frequency of their interactions with you.

2. Clearly explain what's changing (and why) in a way that is relevant to your clients and highlights how this will benefit them.

3. Recognize that not everyone will love the changes you make.

4. When you do ask clients to decide whether to stay with you or move elsewhere, follow up in a timely fashion and get a definite answer.

5. If you do allow exceptions to your process or accept clients who fall outside your ideal profile, ensure you have compelling reasons that make sense in light of your overall business objectives.

6. Remain professional and keep good notes.

A solid financial services business is built on strong relationships. You want to do business with people who respect you, value your advice, and are willing to listen. If people don't want to take that approach, you don't want them as clients. If possible, don't bring them into your business to start with. If they are already clients and you need to do some streamlining, weed them out. It's not always easy, but it's worth the effort to get control of your business so you can be successful and enjoy what you do. You will develop a deeper conviction for your process and approach, and that will attract the kind of clients you want to do business with.

Each of the steps you have taken so far is important in gaining control of the structure of your business. With your investment and client-servicing processes in place and your book filling with clients who fit the way you work, the next challenge is to gain and maintain control of your time. In the next chapter, we'll look at how to focus on doing the best things at the right time.

CHAPTER EIGHT
GET THE CRUCIAL THINGS DONE

"The key is not to prioritize what's on your schedule,
but to schedule your priorities."

− STEPHEN COVEY, EDUCATOR, BUSINESSMAN, AND AUTHOR OF
THE SEVEN HABITS OF HIGHLY EFFECTIVE PEOPLE

I f you don't deliberately identify your priorities and assign specific times to accomplish those activities, distractions will constantly pull you off track and you will struggle with:

- People's urgent desires that conflict with your own goals

- Giving your attention to compellingly presented but noncritical information

- Trying to focus on too many things

- Frustration at never getting to the things that can move your business forward

Building and successfully managing your advisory business takes time. But, you can achieve the success you want sooner when you know what is most important to get done *and* you do it. Identifying and completing your priorities moves you toward your ultimate objectives, which means the rewards of your work are closer at hand.

We all know priorities are those things that are most important to do. But in reality, we often treat priorities as good ideas that we'll get to once we have a spare moment (which very rarely magically appears). If you are responsible for planning your time, key activities get completed. Make these priorities the focus of your best energy and concentration. But, consider that not all your activities carry the same level of importance. Are you spending the best part of your day and your best efforts on the most vital things? This chapter will help you focus on getting the crucial things done.

When I was preparing for the Olympics my main objective each day was to take my body to the point of absolute physical exhaustion and then train myself to mentally move through that exhaustion and make my body keep going. (It's not an approach I recommend applying to life in general!) Because I demanded so much of my body and mind, rest was a top priority. So, at 21 years old I had a strict 8:30 pm bedtime.

I also had a great rapport with many New Zealand journalists. We enjoyed talking about what was happening on the world swimming scene and about the hopes and performances of the Kiwi team members. Most of the guys I talked to regularly knew my routine and respected it. When a reporter called at 8:10 at night, we'd have a good conversation for 20 minutes. However, if someone called at 8:35, he would get my mum and she had a double black belt in gatekeeping! I remember the time a world record was broken at some overseas meet and a reporter wanted a comment from me for the morning news bulletin. The reporter tried his best to get past Mum, telling her he was sure I'd be happy to help him out this one time because it wasn't *that* late, it would be *really* quick, and he *urgently* needed a sound bite for the morning news. Each protestation from him was only met with deeper resolve from my mother. When this type of encounter happened I'd call back early the next day, mention that Mum had said he really needed to get through to me, and ask how I could help. Invariably, the morning shift reporter would say he just wanted to catch up with me, see how my training was going, and get my response to the new world record—that "it wasn't anything *urgent.*"

Because the reporter who called at night had wanted something from me, he presented the issue as *urgent* when it was simply *convenient* for him if I would give him my immediate attention. Access to me the next day before I left for morning training, when it was convenient to me, was just as acceptable as speaking to me at 8:35 the night before.

People like instant gratification, so it's understandable that when they want something from you, getting it sooner feels more satisfying to them than having to wait. They'll often ask for your focus when it suits their timetable. Recognize this: *If you fail to prioritize your time, other people will.* Immediately responding to others' requests feels like the polite, friendly, or kind thing to do, and so we rarely evaluate if it is an *important* thing to do in that particular moment. If you are not firmly fixed on beginning and completing the most important things *you* need to do, other people's ideas, agendas, and deadlines will monopolize your time, you'll likely not even notice, and your priorities will suffer as a result.

WHY DO I KEEP GETTING SO DISTRACTED?

Distractions come in all guises, shapes, and sizes. Often when I begin working with advisors they're frustrated with themselves for repeatedly giving in to distractions, which they know are keeping them from the best activities. I frequently hear, "I'm not sure why I do this." Avoiding distractions is typically about more than summoning up additional self-control or simply trying harder. Understanding and addressing some key underlying issues that fuel distraction can help you keep focused.

Lack of Conviction for Your Process

Without vivid pictures of your end goals and clearly identified elements of the process that will move you toward those goals, you'll likely lack the conviction you need to consistently overcome distractions. Psychologists say a large part of the focus we desire relies on keeping irrelevant things from coming into focus.[1] Without strong conviction for your process and the resulting commitment to targeted activities, shutting down the impulse to give in to distractions can become almost impossible. Distractions that seem sensible and often take very little effort to justify are the hardest to resist.

Perhaps you have set aside the afternoon for reviewing your model investment portfolios and have been working diligently for a couple of hours. You're starting to feel fatigued and so decide to take a break and glance at some LinkedIn emails that came through earlier in the day. (You figure it reduces the stack of emails in your inbox and it's still business focused.) You see a link to an article titled, "Seven Mistakes Every Financial Advisor Must Avoid," and you click on it. After all, it *is* related to your business and you might pick up some helpful information. Then that article has a couple of other interesting, related links, so you check those out, too. Suddenly it's 20 minutes later and you still need to finish rebalancing your portfolios.

When you're starting to feel fatigued, taking a mental break to refresh is a good idea. And, there's nothing wrong with looking at social media or even reading interesting business-relevant articles. Each step seemed reasonable. But, if rebalancing portfolios was your priority during that time period and you let your focus shift to reading articles instead (no matter how useful or relevant), taking that break was a distraction.

Obvious distractions, such as letting a quick break in the middle of the workday afternoon turn into an hour of video games on your phone, are clearly immaterial to the work at hand and take relatively little effort to recognize and avoid. However, seemingly sensible activities, such as reading business-focused articles, reviewing market commentary, or updating CRM information, can be the sneakiest of distractions. They're hard to spot because they may actually be good things to do. But, even the right things if done at the wrong time become distractions.

Reviewing your inbox is good, but not if it's keeping you from time you've allocated to prepare for a client's review meeting. Staying current with what's happening to markets globally and remaining abreast of the Federal Reserve's activities are useful, because you may strategically use this information during client reviews. However, endlessly listening to random analysts or scrolling through headlines in the name of research, when you already have a couple of good commentaries from analysts you like and follow, is a time-wasting distraction. Reviewing the historical performance of a mutual fund you are considering including in your portfolios is wise, but not if your priority was speaking with a client's CPA to get information about tax consequences of a possible change to the client's investment holdings.

If you are committed to six specific action steps that you know will definitely lead you to reaching your objective, it is much easier to identify a seventh activity and jettison it as a distraction (no matter how sensible it seems). You can see that it's not among your specified activities, so it should not be important to you because giving time to it will only cause you to lose focus and delay your progress toward completing your identified six priority actions. As we covered in Chapter 3, deadlines can be very useful in helping you remain focused on your priorities, simply because you do not have time to explore every possible option. There will be other possible—and perhaps even good—routes to your end goals. But when you pick your path and develop conviction for your process, you know what to do now *and* what to do next to keep you moving toward your goal. You have clear guardrails to keep you on track, allowing you to more clearly see the difference between what is relevant and what is merely interesting.

KEY ISSUES THAT FUEL DISTRACTION

- Lack of conviction for your process

- Competition for your attention

- Undervaluing small activities

- Denying that something really is a distraction

- Not sticking to a schedule

Competition for Your Attention

Another challenge to staying on track is the sheer volume of material available that is specifically designed to grab your attention. Being constantly connected to the world is the norm today, and it is increasingly harder to keep focused on just one thing in the midst of the multitasking swirl that surrounds us. As an example, it's no longer enough to watch a talking head deliver the news—we're bombarded by quickly changing pictures to look at, crawlers that introduce completely unrelated information, stock prices or sports scores, not to mention the flashing invitations to text or tweet our thoughts about it all. Just catching up on the headlines can be exhausting! So much of the information at our fingertips is specifically designed to distract us from what we're looking for. The fact that our brains are wired to pay attention to novel information and experiences makes tuning out all this stimuli particularly difficult, to the point that we often feel anxious we're missing something really important.[2]

Staying focused requires physical energy. Our brains consume glucose when concentrating, which includes ignoring irrelevant information and shutting down extraneous impulses. And much like any other muscle exerting sustained effort, your brain gets tired exercising the self-control needed to focus. Each time you resist a distraction you consume a limited resource, making it increasingly more difficult to sustain your focus by resisting further distractions.[3] If you are constantly bombarded with demands for your attention—email notifications, a ringing phone, colleagues at your door, random thoughts about activities that need to be done—each one of those reduces your ability to keep locked on to what you were trying to accomplish in the first place. Again, without clear priorities to help shut out demands for your attention to unnecessary things, your resistance will get drained away and you'll be more likely to give in to time-sapping, unproductive distractions.

Undervaluing Small Activities

We also slow down our progress because we underestimate the cumulative value of doing small things consistently. A few minutes lost here or there, 15 minutes to help a colleague brainstorm ideas, and another six minutes in the break room chatting each individually seem inconsequential over the course of a day. You tell yourself it'll only take a second, not clearly seeing the cost of those small distractions and giving yourself unconscious permission to indulge them. Giving in to the distractions becomes a habit, as you regularly spend your precious attention, time, and energy on trivial things. Reaching your goals takes so much longer than you anticipated, which leaves you frustrated and disappointed.

When I present to groups, I often show a video of my Olympic swim. With less than four meters to go in the 200-meter race, Sergei Zabolotnov, the swimmer who eventually placed fourth, was clearly ahead of me. With only three strokes left, from the center of the pool he glanced to his right and caught sight of me in lane one. All of us in that backstroke final had spent years training what to do in those last meters of the race: keep your head straight and charge for the wall. At the very end of the race when he was tired, all that training was overridden in a split-second as he turned his head to look. Then on his last stroke into the wall, which he started before I started my last stroke, he glanced again, and it cost him an Olympic medal. Two brief, seemingly insignificant glances changed the outcome of the race and our lives. I'm not criticizing Zabolotnov. He was an outstanding swimmer and had even held the world record in our event. I tell the story to emphasize that if one of the world's fastest, greatest, most highly trained athletes can be distracted when it matters most, any of us can be distracted too. Little things do matter, and resisting distractions requires constant, deliberate, and determined action.

Not Recognizing Distractions

Once you identify your priorities, many distractions become obvious. Regularly going to a local networking group's meeting is clearly not a productive use of your time if you can see that your target prospects are not there. Spending hours planning, preparing for, and presenting educational seminars to find new clients is unmistakably wasted effort if only a couple of your existing clients attend every time. Yes, by all means experiment when building your business, but be honest about what is working and what isn't. However, distractions that are part of your everyday environment can be much more difficult to spot. Because you have always done something or done it in a particular way, it can become such an accepted part of the atmosphere you simply don't notice that it is unnecessarily consuming your focus.

In the 1980s competitive road cyclists started paying attention— literally—to their atmosphere. For over a century they had focused on cardiovascular fitness and muscular strength, but their equipment didn't change significantly. As technology developed in the area of aerodynamics, cyclists realized the very air around them was creating resistance and costing them time. Obviously the air was not going to go away, so they had to figure out how to move through it differently to reduce the drag. Aero helmets with pointy tails, one-piece Lycra skinsuits, and aero bars that more easily keep the body in a crouched, aerodynamic position became required racing equipment, and speeds increased. What distracting elements are you so immersed in that it's hard to see another way is possible?

After hearing me speak about this, Mark committed to looking at every element of his business from a different angle. One of the first changes he made was getting rid of the financial TV channel on his computer. From his earliest days in the financial industry, having financial programs on in the background was the "done thing" in all the offices he had worked in. Not only did it seem to make sense—ensuring he stayed on top of the very latest market activity and heard what commentators were saying firsthand—he had simply never considered another way of operating. When he began thinking differently, he realized the constant chatter was a huge drag on his attention and his emotions. After he removed the website from his list of favorites, he was amazed by the positive difference it made in both his mood and daily productivity.

Email is integral to business operations today, but it is also one of the most ubiquitous distractions. One productivity study reported more than 72 percent of advisors respond to email messages as they come in.[4] The pop-up or dinging notifications are almost irresistible—again, it's intriguing to turn your attention to something new and justify it by wanting to appear responsive to clients and colleagues. While many advisors admit improving how they manage email would limit distractions, it can seem too big of a beast to tame. So they just keep doing what they've been doing. They give in to the habit of continually allowing their attention to be dragged away from other activities, no matter how important those activities are.

There are different ways of taming this beast. Setting specific blocks of time to respond to emails is one of the tools used by the minority of advisors who feel in control of their businesses and their time.[5] When you are focused on other activities, turn off, or at least minimize, your email notifications by setting longer retrieval intervals. There are very few messages that can't wait for a reply, and holding off until you can give an email reply your full attention greatly reduces unintentional, yet still unprofessional and potentially costly typos or other errors.

One thing you can do is resist opening every new email in your inbox when you start your computer first thing in the morning. Glance at anything you've been waiting for or that requires a time-sensitive response, reply where immediately needed, then refocus your energy on other more demanding activities. Maybe you want to use systems or software to help you filter and file what comes in. Some advisors set several limited blocks of time each day to purposefully clear their inbox. Short breaks between longer chunks of focused time can be a great time to switch your focus to quickly scan your inbox, trash irrelevant messages, and see if there is something truly urgent that needs your immediate attention. Most often you'll see that messages can wait until the time you have set aside for giving your undivided attention to writing and sending email responses, resting easy that nothing will be overlooked and can be addressed later. Email isn't going away, but there are ways to control its drag to keep it from controlling you.

Many business teams are in the practice of meeting each morning for everyone to advise what they are working on or make upcoming needs known so the day ahead runs more smoothly. These meetings are meant to be quick overviews but often drag on. One person will mention something that involves another person, and suddenly everyone in the morning huddle is simply observing the two having a protracted conversation about their project. Once permitted, these types of conversations tend to grow in frequency. When time is wasted, team members can become frustrated because they would rather be doing something else. Many teams acquiesce in frustration because they don't see another option for everyone to efficiently communicate, or they give up on the meetings altogether, leading to more frustration when issues arise because someone neglected to tell someone else of their plans or expectations. Again, sometimes a new perspective can help. Electronically sharing calendars among all team members might reduce the need for more detailed, longer meetings. New meeting rules can be established, such as no interruptions when each person is reporting his or her main three important activities for the day. Changes to established routines and habits are possible.

Take a new look at how you operate the daily activities of your business. What few changes could make significant differences to how efficiently you work? Don't get trapped into ignoring or justifying ineffective practices just because you have always done it that way or because you believe you can't realistically stop doing certain activities. This rigid thinking ensures you will be dragged down in your efforts to reach your goals. Take a new perspective. Be willing to consider that there might be a better way to operate.

Not Sticking to a Schedule

The most significant obstacle keeping people from making real progress toward their goals is not sticking to a schedule. We were trained to operate on a schedule and lived the first couple of decades of our lives doing specific activities at designated times. If we stuck to our routines over the years, consistently doing specific activities at determined times, we likely managed to get a tremendous amount of work done, mostly on time and often with great results.

When we started our careers and were taking on the greatest responsibilities, challenges, and distractions we had ever faced, most of us began to rethink our tested, time-blocked, and structured routines. Some of those childhood and teenage schedules became less relevant as we moved on in life, and we may have discounted what those time-blocked schedules allowed us to do. But don't make the mistake of abandoning the valuable time management tools of schedules and routines when you need them the most to effectively address priorities and produce remarkable achievements.

THE MYTH OF MULTITASKING

Many people balk at the suggestion of time-blocking their day, saying it's just not realistic in the "real world." They say the demands on them are so plentiful that they really have no choice except to constantly do things as they come up just to get through each day. My response is: Are you achieving what you want to achieve? Are you getting done the things you've identified you need to do to succeed, or are you just busy and feeling frazzled? Typically, people who feel the busiest and insist on the need to constantly multitask are not satisfied with what they are getting done because they aren't achieving the goals they've established for themselves.

The concept of multitasking comes from the world of computing and originally referred to a computer processor simultaneously executing multiple tasks. As our lives have become more complex with more to do each day, the notion of multitasking sounded like a good way to approach the human condition, and our culture bought into the concept. Study after study now says human multitasking is a myth because our brains are simply not set up to simultaneously process and focus on multiple tasks. The reality is, you can't simultaneously have an appointment with a prospect and fill out ACAT forms from a previous meeting earlier in the day. You can't rebalance a client's portfolio while having a phone discussion with another client about his upcoming retirement. Instead, multitasking ends up meaning quickly switching focus back and forth from one activity to another—usually unsuccessfully. Research says that working this way makes us less productive and less accurate, less creative, less able to determine what is irrelevant, and less able to control our emotions.[6,7]

It even changes our brain in ways that make it harder to focus.[8] The good news is that the changes aren't irreparable: we can retrain our brains to unitask—that is, to do one thing at a time, the opposite of multitasking. Unitasking actually allows you to get more done with higher quality.[9] So, how do you realistically do this in the real world?

First, determine what specific activities you need to be doing. If one of your goals is to acquire eight clients, each with $500,000 or more in assets, within the next 12 months, you will need to find and bring on board two of these people every three months. You identified your objective and deadline in your TARGET Goal, and you have broken down your numbers so you know what you need to accomplish at checkpoints along the way. Now, connect your daily activities to that goal. Where will you find these new clients? How will you meet them? How will you get the opportunity to talk with them about their financial needs and let them know how you help people like them? The Distraction-Proof Pathway sheet is a helpful tool to lay out your actionable steps. (You can see a sample in Figure 8.1 and also download sheets to fill out and learn more about this tool at www.DPAresources.com.)

TARGET Goal	Goal Reaching Priorities	Benefits & Results
To acquire new client assets of $10 million within the next 12 months ($835,000 per month)	• Consistently offer availability to clients' friends and family (6–8 per week) • Increase centers of influence (2 meetings/month) • Cold-walk Thursday & Friday afternoons • Effectively use CRM system—notes, comments, etc.	• Enough income to take a 4 day weekend mini-vacation with my spouse each quarter • Begin college funding for my children • Funds to find and remunerate best quality support staff

Figure 8.1 Distraction-Proof Pathway Sample

In order to find your new clients, your priority activities might include attending events for small business owners to meet new people in your target market, being more proactive in asking current clients for referrals (using the recommended wording we've covered previously), developing relationships with other professionals who could be referral partners, or cold-walking downtown. Often advisors anticipate a list of an overwhelming number of things to do, but when they start naming specific actions to take, they see that the key is not doing a lot of different things but repeating *and completing* a specific core of productive activities over and over. Develop a list of limited, realistic, and achievable activities. When you can clearly see what you need to do, you know where to focus your time and attention and can make an immediate start. Identifying these activities makes distractions more obvious, so you can stay on track to achieve what you want sooner. Seeing your activities in direct relation to the benefits you'll enjoy when you reach your goals, as the Distraction-Proof Pathway sheet allows, will help keep you accountable to those priorities.

We all have the same amount of time each day. The people who achieve a lot and stay calm as they complete task after task typically have routines that guide their days. They appropriate their attention, focus, and effort on specific tasks at specific times. Then they protect that time from outside intrusions, deliberately working through one task after another, which keeps them on pace to reach their objectives. The thought that you do not have enough time to focus on only one thing at a time is a fallacy. It takes your brain time to switch from one task to another, so if you are doing that constantly with only very short bursts of focus on any particular task, as happens in multitasking, you lose a tremendous amount of productive time each day. It is actually quicker to simply do one thing at a time.[10]

Time-block your day, with segments of your schedule devoted to acting on your key priorities. I typically aim to sit at my desk and focus on a specific task for 50 or 55 minutes. I set the timer on my phone and then work solidly for that time. Then I take a break for 5 to 10 minutes, unless I'm only 5 to 10 minutes away from completing a task, in which case I'll keep working and take a break when I'm finished. (Using the timer to keep yourself honest about your break time as well as your work time can be very useful.) I might quickly scan emails or listen to voice mail messages. I often like to get up from my desk and move around, whether it's going to the kitchen to refill my water bottle or taking a quick walk around the block. By consistently taking short breaks each hour, even if I don't really feel like it, I can stay fresh and focused over the course of a whole day.

Here's what a typical time-blocked week might look like. (See Figure 8.2.) Of course this is an ideal, and you may need to be somewhat flexible, but having most of your time planned will make you much more productive than simply addressing things as they come up.

You can create your own calendar or log in to www.DPAresources.com to download a blank calendar template you can fill in with your personal schedule and see further details about time-blocking.

Mark out appropriate times to do things that move you toward realizing your dreams. Set appointments for these activities before your week begins and treat those times with as much importance as A-client appointments. Time-blocking eliminates the paralysis you can experience when you are overwhelmed by your workload. Because you know that the vital activities you need to do have been scheduled, you reduce the stress that comes from trying to keep a multitude of things on your mind.

Notes		Monday	Tuesday	Wednesday	Thursday	Friday
	5:00 AM					
		Breakfast, shower, dress				
	6:00 AM	Personal / family time				
		Commute to office				
	7:00 AM	Review day, week & prep for meetings				
	8:00 AM		Any follow-up from yesterday's mtgs or calls			
	9:00 AM	Staff mtg				
	10:00 AM		Client / prospect appts			
		15-min walk; check email, answer phone calls				
	11:00 AM	Client / prospect appts				
	12:00 PM	Client / prospect appts				
	1:00 PM	Lunch; walk; check email / phone messages				
		Insert notes into CRM from morning meetings				Client appts
	2:00 PM	Research / develop material to send clients	Develop alliance relationships	Research / develop material to send clients	Marketing activities	Send client materials
	3:00 PM	Client / prospect appts			Cold-walking	Review for mtgs nxt wk, clear desk, org 3 items
	4:00 PM	Follow-up from today's appts, CRM notes, market research				Gym
		Clear desk, organize 3 items to do tomorrow				
	5:00 PM	Gym				
	6:00 PM					
	7:00 PM	Home, dinner, personal / family time				
	8:00 PM					
	9:00 PM	Computer off, light reading, go to bed				

Figure 8.2 Typical Time–Blocked Week

USE YOUR TIME STRATEGICALLY

You will always have more mundane things to attend to, and because they seem simple it can be tempting do those items first. But if you know you are most able to concentrate in the morning, when your energy and ability to focus are at their highest levels, setting aside uninterrupted time to do activities that require more focused thought and creativity is a much better use of your limited time. Set a time for paperwork or other more mundane tasks that take less concentration at another time of the day.

Try to set client meetings for the time of day when you are most alert and ready to listen. Discipline yourself to take clear enough notes during your meetings to allow you to enter details into your contact management system later when your energy is lower, so that you don't spend your prime time doing data entry. Of course, the administrative activities still need to be done, but don't let these less-demanding tasks take time that would be better devoted to your priority actions. Strategically *schedule* time for both types of activity. Passively expecting extra time and energy to randomly appear so you can finally devote focus to working on your priorities guarantees you'll be frustrated and stressed. Instead, purposefully plan how you will use your time and focus.

If one of your priorities is building strategic referral partnerships, book time on your calendar to do some online research to find a few estate attorneys, divorce lawyers, or CPAs in your area. Perhaps your Internet research will take less mental focus than other activities in your day and would be good to do after 3:30 in the afternoon. Ensure you stick to the task at hand, however, and don't just "quickly check" social media and end up spending the time you had allocated for researching potential referral partners reading articles about helping clients with retirement planning. After your research on these centers of influence is done, calendar times to make contact. Perhaps you want to send them a handwritten note to introduce yourself, enclosing an article about a timely topic or an area where you could be of particular assistance to them or their clients. Then, block out time to follow up by phone to see if meeting face-to-face would be productive.

If you want to cold-walk, get intentional with your scheduling. Thursday afternoons are an especially good time for this: business owners are typically more relaxed with the weekend in sight but still in business mode and more willing to engage with you. Friday afternoons when the workweek is ending is also a time when people feel freer to talk. So, perhaps you want to calendar walking times for Thursday and Friday afternoons from 2:30 to 4:00. Practice what you will say, stick to your timetable, and start walking.

A short window on Monday mornings can be a good time to look ahead at what client meetings you have scheduled for the week. Review portfolio material, gather and prepare necessary documents, and make notes about points you want to cover during the appointment at this time when you're fresh and can think more deeply about how to maximize your time with particular clients. If a client is passionate about a specific sports team or hobby, spend a few minutes coming up to speed with a way you can connect with them over this personal interest. If clients accidentally mix up the day or time of their appointment and show up early (it happens sometimes, even with clear and timely communication from your end confirming appointment details), you'll still be prepared for an effective meeting.

You might want to allocate time-blocks every couple of weeks to find and read articles about relevant financial issues. This can be helpful in deepening your own knowledge so you can speak to prospects and clients with confidence in your expertise. Save good-quality, informative pieces to build your own resource library, so you have material on hand about topics like Social Security, Medicare, college costs and 529 plans, budgeting, and estate and end-of-life planning. You can quickly send copies of these articles as follow-ups to casual conversations with clients and prospects to show you are thinking of them and are a source of valuable, relevant information.

If you've constructed your own portfolios using 8 or 10 different funds, block time to talk with your wholesalers. Do this regularly so they'll get used to your driving the relationship and won't pursue you too often. As you build a relationship and they get to know your interests, they'll likely be eager to provide helpful information that's pertinent to you, making your time with them relevant and productive.

If you've attended a training class, you might want to gather a group of advisors to form a mastermind group. You could block time for a conference call each month to share business ideas and information about what's working or what's not. As an added bonus, you might learn to use a teleconference or web-conference system to meet with your colleagues, which you can then comfortably and confidently use to conduct remote client meetings.

You can even set time-blocks for giving in to distractions. (Yes, you read that correctly!) As I mentioned earlier, a lot of things that may distract you aren't bad in and of themselves; they become distractions when they get your attention at the wrong time. This is even true for unproductive, non-work-related activities. If you have been working solidly for an hour, take a five-minute break. Hold yourself to only five minutes, but go ahead and use that time to text your friend about upcoming weekend plans, call your spouse to say hi, or glance at Facebook. Use the "distraction" as a reward for staying on task for the previous hour. Give yourself a mental break, have a bit of fun, and laugh—guilt-free. It will refresh you and leave you more ready to focus on your next priority activity.

TIME-BLOCKING CHALLENGES

Despite all the benefits of planning periods of uninterrupted focus for specific activities, the concept of time-blocking is often a change that people are reluctant to make. Here are some of the most common challenges I've heard followed by my responses.

Time-blocking is too rigid; it doesn't leave me with enough flexibility to plan my overall week. Each week brings its own, unique demands for your time. That's why, before you start your week, it's important for you to know the core business-building activities you need to get done. By scheduling those activities into your week as unbreakable appointments, you will ensure they get done and still have available blocks of time for other activities.

For example, if you want to have 10 prospect meetings each week because you know you have a great conversion rate from face-to-face meetings, allocate time for these. If you have decided to structure your business schedule so you do not have meetings on Fridays unless there truly is no other option, set aside a total of 10 blocks of time Monday through Thursday. Sixty minutes is a good amount of time to plan for: a productive 50-minute exploratory meeting and then, if you both want to work together, for the remaining 10 minutes after your time with your prospect make follow-up notes and plan for your next in-depth meeting. There will still be plenty of time for other activities during the week. By putting these time holds in your calendar several weeks ahead of time, you'll keep the pressure on yourself to keep hunting for prospects. The process ensures that meeting with prospects is not an abstract idea stuck on your planning documents—you've allocated real time in your calendar to do it.

So many things can happen in a day to throw off my schedule that it's just not worth the effort to plan one in the first place. Unplanned things will always come up. Time-blocking gives you a mechanism to evaluate the interruptions and determine if they are urgent enough to respond to immediately, or if replying later when it is more convenient for you is just as acceptable. Try to protect your planned, focused time from interruptions. However, occasionally there will be urgent issues that truly do require your immediate attention—a question from your compliance team, a request from a client's CPA, or transferring cash from clients' brokerage accounts into their checking accounts, for example. While these urgent activities may not directly contribute to moving you closer to your end objectives sooner, addressing them directly is prudent if putting them off means poor service or greater time-consuming delays later on. If you do get sidetracked, time-blocking helps make the diversions temporary. Because you know what you *should* be focused on during that time, you can quickly take care of the pressing matter demanding your attention and then immediately return to your key activity. Once in a while, you may need to be available at any time for a couple of days, such as when you are helping a client interface with a bank and title company regarding closing a deal on a home purchase. On the rare occasion when you must completely switch your focus to an unplanned activity over a longer period of time, having a set agenda lets you see what did not get done and where you can reprogram it back into your schedule so nothing gets forgotten.

When my clients want to talk to me they expect (and deserve) my immediate attention; after all, it's* their *money. Relationships include being flexible, accessible, and friendly, yet you can't effectively serve your clients if you are always in reaction mode. Answering your phone immediately every time it rings is not necessarily great service. Great service happens most when you address your client's needs and concerns thoroughly. When you time-block your day, ensure you schedule regular times for returning phone calls. Clients rarely have needs that can't wait an hour or two. Once you listen to their message, you'll have time to gather any necessary information and be fully prepared to give them a more thorough and succinct answer than if they had unexpectedly caught you in the midst of some other activity.

When you take on a new client, explain your system to them (especially when you are in the startup phase of your business and don't yet have an assistant who can receive their calls). Clarify that just as they are receiving your undivided attention during their meeting with you, you may not be immediately available when they call if you are meeting with someone else. Reassure them, though, that you will get back to them within a short period of time. Encourage them to leave detailed messages for you so that you'll have the information they want or know what they would like you to do as soon as you're available.

If you have an assistant or partner who may receive calls when you're not available, introduce clients to them immediately after their first meeting with you. Let clients know your team members are great at what they do, clearly relay information they receive, and make it easier for you to respond at the first opportunity. Assure clients they can explain what they want to your associates if they happen to reach one of them instead of you.

If you have a client who is anxious about your not always being immediately available, be aware that you are dealing with a demanding person who may have unreasonable expectations of you in the future. Lay out how you work and what they can expect from you early in your relationship. If you need to wean yourself off responding to clients immediately, let the phone go to voice mail, listen to the message (so you assure yourself it does not demand your immediate attention), make a note of it, then forget about it and get back to what you need to do. You can respond during your next break.

I don't like to micromanage each part of my day. Time-blocking isn't micromanaging; it's planning to ensure you get the important things done. Your priorities form the framework for all your other activities to hang off of. They dictate your direction, focus, and actions. Recognize that if you are not willing to plan your days, you will be vulnerable to all sorts of distractions. Prioritizing identifies *what* must be done; time-blocking establishes *when* what must be done *will* be done.

If you say something is important, take the responsibility to set aside the time to do it. A perfectly time-blocked week is an ideal, and there will be times when you'll need to make adjustments. If you won't time-block, scale back your dreams or accept they'll take longer to achieve. There is far too much to do in this industry to believe it will all be done in the most productive, helpful order without deliberate scheduling. Some outstanding individual might make some progress for a while juggling things as they arise, but consider how much more they could get done, with less stress, if they were willing to be more focused, deliberate, and disciplined about how they used their time. Experiment with managing your schedule with time-blocking and see what works for you.

DISTRACTION-PROOF STEPS

1. Complete the Distraction-Proof Pathway sheet to identify your priorities.

2. Rank your priority activities and assess the time and energy needed for each one.

3. Time-block your week.

4. Commit to keeping your schedule.

Identify your priorities, schedule time to take action, and see things through to completion. Trust that doing one thing at a time will make you more productive. You'll not only realize your dreams, but you'll be more relaxed and enjoy success sooner because you will avoid stress-inducing distractions that will derail you from where you want to go.

As we've touched on in this chapter, there is a lot to do when you are building a successful advisory business. Sometimes, even with the best plans and systems small doubts about your ability to effectively do what it takes can creep in. Left unchecked this self-doubt can become a debilitating distraction. The next chapter will discuss how to handle those thoughts and keep them from sabotaging your great work.

CHAPTER NINE

SLAY THE SELF-DOUBT DRAGON

*"Our doubts are traitors, and make us lose the good
we oft might win, by fearing to attempt."*

– WILLIAM SHAKESPEARE, POET, PLAYWRIGHT, AND ACTOR,
IN *MEASURE FOR MEASURE*, ACT I, SCENE IV

Having some doubts and fears about succeeding in this industry should not surprise you. However, if you give too much attention to your concerns, you'll be distracted by:

- Constantly second-guessing yourself

- Imagining negative scenarios (which rarely ever happen) that sap your emotional energy

- Skewed perspectives, causing you to lose sight of what really matters in your business

- Procrastination to avoid the potential failure you fear

Growing a business can be daunting at times. On the outside you appear to be doing fine, yet internally you are encountering unsettling little air pockets on your journey to success—some bumpy self-doubt turbulence and occasional confidence-draining headwinds. Whether you're new to the business or you've been in it for several years, take heart: wondering if you truly have what it takes to succeed in this industry isn't unusual.

One day a voice from somewhere in the back of your mind pipes up, demanding to know what right you have to manage other people's money and advise them about making key life-changing decisions. "Just who do you think you are?" it asks. "How much do you really know? Just how good do you think you've become?" If left unchecked, that voice can take on a life of its own and develop into a little gremlin that climbs up on your shoulder and nestles close to your ear, whispering to you just before a meeting, "Why would you think these people should give you their hard-earned money and place their lifelong dreams in your hands? What if you mess up? What if you make a mistake? Remember Uncle Pete and the suggestions you gave to him? Remember how that went? South, if I recall. By the way, how are those quartile class rankings holding up for you?"

Knowing where these distracting, challenging internal voices stem from will help you to silence them and refocus on building your business. In this chapter we're going to look at how to deal with self-doubt before it distracts you and interferes with your business.

My biggest self-doubts when I started in this business stemmed from growing up in another country. I was not raised with the U.S. economy and financial system as part of my cultural backdrop. I was concerned about how older prospects would feel about having someone with an accent manage their finances and talk cogently about U.S. markets, investment details, and financial planning issues. Would they see me as an outsider and mentally keep me pegged there? While they might have seemed interested in why I came to the United States (that would be through a swimming scholarship at the University of California at Berkeley) and my Olympic experience, would they see me as just the sports guy who was fun to talk with but not as a knowledgeable, credible person to manage their intimate financial affairs?

You likely began this career with a vision of building a profitable business by helping people plan their financial future. Remember that initial thrill you felt when a great prospect said how much they'd enjoyed talking with you? You felt high, giddy with potential and excitement. Perhaps it's been a while since you had a meeting where you felt like you really connected with a prospect, and you've been hearing a few more nos than yeses lately. Disappointment can turn to doubt as you start asking yourself, "Can I actually do this?" When you start feeling vulnerable you may dwell on your doubts, thinking, "Who was I kidding? There are so many things I don't know. Building this business is going to take so long. So many people already have an advisor they're happy with; why would they work with me?" Rapidly, your emotions and thoughts can start spiraling, feeding the growing negative, self-sabotaging voices that are taking a lot of your focus. You're left discouraged, disillusioned, and deciding next month may be your last in this business.

The fuel for this negative thinking often has little to do with the reality of current circumstances. You came to this career carrying your own emotional paradigms and decades of life experiences. Ideally, you had a dream childhood, growing up with consistent, positive encouragement from your parents and others close to you. Perhaps you've made a habit of succeeding at all you've attempted in life, and you see this business as the next challenge to master. If that describes your background and thinking, that's wonderful; make sure you thank those who have been on your support team.

Often, however, the picture is more complicated and not so idyllic. Maybe you feel you never received encouragement when you were younger, even when you desperately yearned for it. You may have had overbearing parents who were trying to deal with their own issues when giving time to you should have been their top priority. Perhaps you grew up with a parent who couldn't handle the thought of your succeeding because he or she needed to be the center of attention and so continually discouraged you in what you tried to do. Or maybe that parent just had a negative outlook on life and communicated that great success only happens to a select few so you would not be disappointed or hurt.

Obstructive mental soundtracks can also have their roots outside your family of origin. Overly negative feedback from a teacher you admired and respected may have left deep impressions. Perhaps a supercritical manager made cutting, demeaning comments that stuck with you. Maybe you have been around pessimistic people who have a knack for spreading the gloom that seems to follow wherever they go. Or maybe it was a colleague who always seemed to have another discouraging story about the trials and tribulations of this industry.

The school yard refrain that sticks and stones may break your bones but words will never hurt you is just not true. Words are powerful. When used negatively (especially by someone you love, trust, and respect), they can traumatize emotions and injure spirits. Being called stupid, worthless, or incompetent can cut deeply. While physical wounds can be immediately assessed and treated to encourage effective healing, harsh words can leave invisible internal wounds, which more often go untreated. In the same way, these untreated emotional wounds can fester and cause problems way beyond the original injury, never properly healing.

Instead of rejecting rash words, people can accept them as valid, which then distorts their sense of self-worth and potential. Over time, people can develop the mistaken belief that they will inevitably, eventually fail because of who they think they really are. They insulate themselves in a small comfort zone, reluctant to try new things or prone to procrastination in order to put off the imagined unavoidable disappointment that lies ahead. Instead of vividly visualizing great outcomes and rewarding results they might reach through diligent work, self-doubts bombard them, and they see potential downsides all too clearly and quickly. Investing time, emotion, energy, or money into anything becomes too big of a risk. If they do finally muster enough courage to take a chance and then start experiencing some success, they live in fear that sooner or later people will find out they are simply frauds who have been fooling everyone with their appearance of competence and achievement. If this sounds closer to your background and thinking than the ideal described above, keep reading.

TIME AND CHANCE

Don't think you're strange or weak if you have some doubt or fear of the unknown. Many very successful advisors can recount days of distress, or even panic, when their calendar had far fewer appointments than they needed and people were not returning their cold calls. We like the security of guarantees; we want to know what will happen and when. But life doesn't necessarily cooperate. We may not have guarantees, but we're not subject to the whim of luck. In fact, there is no such thing as luck. Both good and lousy things can just happen to anyone at any time. Even if you choose to play things safe, unexpected things can still happen. Our attitudes toward what happens are often much more significant than the circumstances themselves.

Rather than asking, "What if I miss?" ask, "What if I make it?" Instead of asking yourself if you have what it takes to succeed in this challenging industry, find out what you believe it does take and then ask yourself if you're prepared to do that. Regardless of your circumstances and actions, time will still tick by. With no effort you're not likely to gain much. So, why not see what you can do? Take advantage of the chances that arise. There's no guarantee everything will turn out perfectly, but you'll certainly accomplish a lot more than if you had not tried anything at all. Don't let the uncertainty of the outcome stop you from taking your first step. Some of life's most rewarding moments require risking being vulnerable. When we realistically, directly look at the worst that could happen, it is often not nearly as terrible as we feared it might be. Time is going to pass, so use it to your advantage and try something.

WORRYING ABOUT WHAT OTHERS THINK

Self-doubt and low self-confidence often manifest as worries about what others think of us. It's natural to want to be thought of positively. It feels good to be liked. But when we get overly concerned with what others think, we become anxious and start an internal monologue that gets louder and more dramatic as we imagine circumstances getting progressively worse.

Charles had recently started at a new firm and shared he was having this type of internal conversation during a coaching session: "Mike, my office manager, just asked me if my uncle, Larry, is still coming into the office on Thursday. I've mentioned Larry to him before, and he knows he has a load of cash. What if I can't land Larry as a client? What if I can't even bring in family members? What will Mike think?"

What Mike might be thinking was not the actual question that was concerning Charles the most. The real issue was the two little words that he had silently tacked onto the end of the question: "What will Mike think *of me*?" In fact, Charles was anxious not only about what Mike would think of him but also about what others in the office would think of him. In the face of self-doubt, the emotional internal monologue brings up skepticism about our ability to connect with prospects and operate a successful business, along with the absolute certainty we are gifted prognosticators and mind readers. This was exactly what was happening when Charles and I spoke: he was already assuming his upcoming meeting with his uncle would be unsuccessful and then anticipating how his office manager and successful colleagues would interpret the negative results.

"I mentioned to Mike what a great guy my uncle is, and Mike said he'd pop in and say hi when we were meeting. That means that Mike and Larry will meet," Charles told me with some panic in his voice.

I asked Charles, "What is the worst thing that can happen if your uncle doesn't become a client?"

"If Larry doesn't become a client, Mike is going to wonder how I'll make it here when my own family won't work with me." He worried that Mike would doubt he had what it takes to be a successful advisor.

I pressed further. "How do you categorically know that's what Mike will think?"

"I don't," Charles replied, "but it stands to reason that if you can't get family—who know you—to be your clients, you're not going to get total strangers who don't know you to be clients."

Charles thought that because family members were supposed to be supportive, they should be the easiest to bring on board. In fact, this isn't necessarily true—sometimes family members can be the *most* difficult people to turn into clients because they are determined to keep their financial affairs separate from their personal relationships. He reasoned that if he could not successfully influence such an "easy" prospect, Mike would assume Charles's uncle didn't trust him enough to work with him and wonder why. Charles had already told himself that Mike would question his ability to convince anyone to become a client and would conclude Charles would fail as an advisor, thus jeopardizing his career. Frequently when self-doubt takes over, any realistic perspective goes out the window.

I asked Charles, "Is the issue getting Larry as a client or are you more concerned about whether total strangers will work with you?"

Charles paused as he considered the question, then answered, "I want people to see me as helpful as a reliable and trustworthy advisor, because I see myself that way as a person. I want people to *want* to work with me."

"Great points," I said. "So let's back up and take both of those statements one at a time. Tell me what your friends thought about your beginning this career."

"They told me they thought I would be ideal for this job. I'm good at looking at the big picture, and they also know I enjoy influencing people to reach their potential," he explained.

"Can you trust your friends, Charles?" I asked.

"Of course!" he was quick to respond. "I spent a lot of time talking about getting into this industry with a couple of my closest buddies. They even pointed out some of the challenges I might face."

"Like what?" I asked.

"Like taking things a little too personally. One of the guys I've stayed close to from college said that learning from negative things that happen and then moving on might be easier said than done for me."

"Interesting point." I continued, "How about your work environment? How do you think others look at you as an advisor?"

"Landing Larry would certainly show them that I can close a prospect. Word has gotten around that he's coming in to meet with me and is giving me a shot at working with him."

I asked Charles what he thought the other advisors might think of him if Larry didn't come on board.

He replied, "One or two would wonder, 'If he can't land family, who can he bring in?' Right? I know some of the others weren't thrilled with Mike giving me an office so soon; a couple of guys had their eye on it for their assistant. I think they might make some comments, wondering if Mike made a wise decision with giving me an office, or even with hiring me in the first place."

"Charles, did Mike ask you about hiring any of these guys?" I asked.

"No, of course he didn't," Charles laughed. "They were here before I was!"

"Right," I agreed. "So let's leave the office politics to Mike and the other advisors and instead focus on what needs to happen for you.

"It seems like you're very much supported by friends and family from what you've told me. Now, before we talk about your wanting people to work with you, tell me why they should. Why should I allow you, Charles, to have influence over me, my hard-earned money, and my greatest dreams and goals?" I challenged him.

"So often I bump into people who haven't had anyone genuinely interested in them as individuals," Charles said. "I truly believe that to most effectively gain someone's trust, you must be interested in their well-being as a person first."

"That's a partial answer, but first and foremost why should I follow you?" I asked.

There was a lengthy pause.

"Because I know how to help," he said.

"Getting closer…but *can* you help?"

"Yes. I know how to help, what to do, and how to communicate that to clients," he replied confidently. "I know I can make a difference in people's lives by helping them get their financial house in order, in helping them plan effectively for retirement."

"That sounds great, Charles. So many people could benefit from that. You need to work with thousands of people!"

"I can't work with everyone," Charles ribbed. "You know when we started together that my goal was to find 48 great clients, remember?"

"That's right; we're looking for your ideal 48. And I think you shared that with Mike, your manager, right? What was his response?"

"He told me that it was a wise, focused way to build a business in this industry," Charles replied.

"Sounds like he might be an advocate for you. Sounds like he might trust your judgment. How long did you say he'd been a manger?"

"Eight years."

"He's probably seen a lot of advisors and their plans, wouldn't you think? And from what you said, he liked your plan, right?"

"Yeah. But what if it doesn't happen?" Charles asked.

"What if it does, Charles?" I countered. "But, for argument's sake, let's just say it doesn't. Let's say that after you've meet with Larry, you decide not to work together. What's going to happen next?"

"I'll need to explain to Mike what happened."

"And what do you think he'll say?"

WHEN THE SELF-DOUBT DRAGON STARTS TO REAR ITS HEAD, REMEMBER:

- **Everyone makes mistakes.** Instead of beating yourself up, learn from what went wrong so you don't repeat that mistake.

- **No one was born an expert in this business.** Everyone had a starting point. Take advantage of opportunities to learn, and over time your expertise will grow.

- **Ask yourself, "What's the worst that can happen?"** Then, realistically answer the question and follow with, "So, what if that *did* actually happen?" Once you identify the worst (and probably highly unlikely) scenario, it can be easier to face and rationally address your fears about that.

- **Attitudes are contagious.** Distance yourself from negative people with pessimistic outlooks who will discourage you.

- **Choose to focus on positive what-ifs.** Ask yourself, "What if I make it?" rather than "What if I fail?"

- **Recognize when you're tired or having a bad day.** Don't take yourself too seriously at these times. It's easy to be overwhelmed by stress and worry when you're feeling physically and emotionally drained. Decide to do something that will refresh you instead of worrying.

- **Leave the popularity game behind.** This isn't high school—it doesn't really matter what others think about you (not that it even mattered back then).

- **Get some objective input.** Seek mentors or coaches who can observe you impartially and help you see both your strengths and weaknesses in a rational light.

"I don't know." Charles's confidence dimmed again.

"How do you not know what Mike will say, yet definitely know what he'll think?"

There was a long pause.

"Charles, you're a great advisor," I assured him. "Here's an exercise to spend a few minutes on today: Ask a couple of the older, more seasoned advisors in your office if they're working with their relatives. Ask them how it's gone for them. If they *are* working with any relatives, ask them how long it took to bring them on. Also, ask Mike about some of the challenges that can come with having relatives as clients and see what advice he has to offer. While you're talking with these people in your office, also ask them if they've landed every prospect they've ever spoken with."

Of course you want to be successful every time you have an opportunity to bring on a new client. But the times when you're not as successful as you would have liked are not a reflection on you as an advisor. Even more important, they're not a reflection on you as a person.

MONITOR YOUR EMOTIONAL TANK'S GAUGE

Modern life can be emotionally charged. Plus, we work in a highly emotive business. As mentioned in Chapter 8, we're more connected than ever and so constantly bombarded by information designed to stand out above the noise and grab our attention. Between heart-wrenching stories, images from wars and global civil strife, and incessant political bickering, it can feel impossible to catch a mental or emotional break. Add to that the daily stress in the equities markets, dramatic headlines, alarming sound bites, and random, unsubstantiated commentary, and it's no wonder we feel so anxious. This environment can be exhausting, and that certainly doesn't help when you're experiencing your own challenging times of doubt.

Recognize the things that drain your emotional "gas tank" and keep situations and people that are more negative and toxic than positive and helpful at arm's length. Don't get trapped into negative office talk. Avoid people who are always condescending to you or others. Avoid people who gossip. Don't engage with or react to inflammatory situations or pessimistic people. Instead, fuel your emotional tank by choosing to be around supportive people who have your interests at heart.

Take deliberate steps to effectively manage your emotions:

- *Don't mindlessly engage in idle, emotional chatter.* Just because something is topical doesn't mean you have to have an opinion or render yours if you do have one.

- *Evaluate carefully what you're reading and watching.* Is it information you need and want, or is it just emotionally based hype that will leave you depleted?

- *Make specific times for refueling.* Be aware of your own emotional state and schedule time to deliberately do things that emotionally and mentally build you up. Maybe it's physical exercise. (I use the time I spend on the elliptical trainer to mentally process things and plan.) Or maybe you feel relaxed and refreshed by doing something creative like playing an instrument or painting. When you keep your emotional tank topped up, you'll find it easier to avoid getting distracted by the unproductive swirl and stay focused on getting to your destination.

- *Listen to your most trusted, closest friends.* Lower your defenses and allow your treasured confidants to have input and influence in your life without having to always have a ready response of your own. Keep a loyal group of supporters close by and use these trustworthy allies to unload apprehensions and help you process limiting negative thinking.

- *Gather groups of supporters.* I had a close relationship with an experienced advisor who I ended up partnering with. She mentored me, encouraged me, and helped me put perceived drawbacks in perspective and use them to my advantage. I trusted her, knowing she had my best interest at heart, and she honestly told me both positive and negative things I needed to hear.

  You may not be looking for a partner, but if you work in an office with other advisors take note of more established advisors who have done well and seem humble and helpful. Talk with them and ask if they'd be interested to mentor you. Ask them if you could meet with them once a week or once every other week for 40 minutes, when it would be convenient for them, to ask them questions. They may even allow you to sit in on meetings they have, where you can observe how they say things and respond to various questions. Often, they'll tell you about the mistakes they made and you'll get to see that these people are human—just like you!

  Also, when I went to company headquarters for three weeks of training before being officially launched as a new advisor, I connected with three others from different parts of the country in the exact same position. We knew we would all be facing similar challenges and decided to form our own mastermind group to share our experiences, ask questions, critique ideas, and encourage one another. We scheduled a conference call with all four of us once a month. We decided our group meetings were not a place to whine about our office managers or the tough economic climate and decided to focus on issues that would help us all grow our businesses. Occasionally, we would ask more experienced advisors to spend time with us and share a challenge they faced when they were getting started and how they overcame it.

- *Take care of yourself.* Know your limitations and be sure you get enough rest, eat well, exercise, and do things you enjoy with people you value. If your negativity or anxiety is oppressive or unmanageable, consider seeking advice from a counselor or medical professional.

ACCENTUATE THE POSITIVE

Acknowledge your doubts. Don't deny them or dismiss them too quickly. While you don't want to let those negative voices grow into a gremlin or an even larger intimidating creature, you do want to evaluate your concerns to determine if they are valid. Reject the false ones immediately and then consider the ones that might relate to genuine challenges. Determine realistic ways to address bona fide issues. Then, after you've processed your doubts let them go and carry on.

Review areas where you are growing and performing strongly. Recognize that even if the actions you are taking are small, they are effectively moving you in the right direction. Give yourself credit for the progress you are making in areas such as developing—and using—a referral system, taking advantage of your CRM system, providing great service, or earning a professional credential. These actions create a strong foundation for the great business you are building.

Keep a "done list." Similar to a to-do list, a done list forces you to keep a daily record of activities and tasks you've *completed*. By recording the things you've accomplished you'll see how productive you've been. You won't finish the day wondering where all your time went or feeling you have nothing to show for it. You'll probably find you're achieving more than you thought you were. You can end your day clear about the progress you've made, feeling great about your efforts and being more focused on where to begin the next morning.

BEATING THE BLUES

Not every day will be perfect. While it would be great to be highly motivated each and every day, some days you're just not going to feel like you can give 100 percent. Often after a presentation, when audiences have heard me recount the hard work necessary to win an Olympic medal, someone will ask if there were days when I just didn't want to go to training. My answer? Absolutely! I had days in the pool when I felt exhausted and sore from the previous day's work, and I *really* did not want to complete my practice.

When these types of days happen for you, don't worry, get frustrated with yourself, or decide to crawl back to bed. You might be tired or disappointed with how a meeting went or have something completely unrelated to work on your mind. Have a fallback process so you don't get too down and waste valuable time wishing you felt differently.

On days when I felt discouraged by my training regime I learned to break my workout into smaller increments. By only focusing on one small element of the workout, I could keep from being overwhelmed by all the work that lay ahead, continue being productive, and get the emotional boost of successfully completing the task at hand. For instance, when I was exhausted, instead of just going through the motions for two hours while I covered hundreds of laps, I'd focus on doing the next six turns well. I'd then give myself a short mental break before focusing on hitting another six turns perfectly. All of a sudden, even though I felt tired, I was doing something really well. Then I'd make a game out of it and see how many perfect turns I could do consecutively. By accomplishing several seemingly small objectives, it didn't take long before I was engaging with the rest of the workout and pushing myself harder than I originally expected to.

If you arrive at your office knowing that your head is just not in the game that day, take on some small objectives and focus on doing those little things well and see them through to completion. Spend 20 minutes clearing your desk, doing some filing, and getting organized. Complete some paperwork that you've been putting off. Pick up the phone and make that call to *one* client. Whatever you focus on, once you have accomplished it, mentally applaud yourself and then determine to complete another small task. Just focus on one thing at a time. So, even when it feels like an off day and you're not at 100 percent, you can leave your office in the evening acknowledging that you still accomplished some useful activities.

DISTRACTION-PROOF STEPS

1. Consider where your negative, sabotaging thoughts are coming from.

2. Gain some perspective by doing something that relieves your stress and refreshes you.

3. Remember your successes.

There will be days that are more challenging than others. Instead of permitting circumstances to deflate you and leave you feeling like you have no control or hope, slow down, realistically self-reflect, and recognize the positive things you have accomplished. Then, determine to take actions, no matter how small, to continue moving yourself forward toward successfully reaching your objectives.

Meetings are where relationships start, and often grow. In the final chapter, we're going to review ways to help ensure productive meetings using processes that will increase your own opportunities for success.

CHAPTER TEN

PUT TOGETHER A WINNING PERFORMANCE

"We are what we repeatedly do. Excellence,
then, is not an act, but a habit."

– WILL DURANT, WRITER, HISTORIAN, AND PHILOSOPHER

Successful meetings are the lifeblood of our business. They are key opportunities to professionally convey the value you offer, the depth of your expertise, and your strong character—all of which help you create loyal, lifelong clients. As you get more experience, your confidence will grow, and you'll feel less nervous as you approach meetings. But don't let your confidence slip into complacency. If you fail to consistently bring your best to every meeting, you'll be distracted by:

- Unexpected last-minute problems that steal your focus

- Worry that clients will ask questions you haven't adequately prepared for

- Edginess and panic from frantic rushing, rather than calm, controlled poise

- Fatigue that hampers your attention and communication

Effective meetings are fundamental to great relationships. It's important to schedule client and prospect meetings for times when you are ready to concentrate and be fully present with those you are meeting with. Clients should feel that they are the sole object of your focus and concern when they are with you. Empathetic and engaged listening is vital. Attention to details is crucial. If you approach any of these meeting elements carelessly, you'll jeopardize your relationship with clients or prospects with whom you want to connect. In this chapter, we'll look closely at the ingredients that create great meetings, moving prospects toward becoming clients and increasing existing clients' confidence in working with you.

Imagine you know that in the next year you will have only 10 prospect meetings, with any new clients coming solely from these appointments. These 10 meetings will be your only opportunities to connect with new people, communicate how you help, and show your capabilities to positively influence your prospects to become your clients. The results of these meetings will directly impact the future growth of your business as well as your personal financial situation. With only 10 occasions to achieve great success, how thoroughly would you prepare? What priority would you give these events, and how focused would your activities be?

Realistically, you'll have many more than 10 opportunities to meet with prospects over the next 12 months. If you are in the early stages of establishing your business, you will *need* many more than 10 meetings to keep your business operational. Regardless of the number of meetings you have during the next year, that number will be finite.

Your opportunities to grow your business and move toward your long-term goals will be limited.

Olympic athletes have limited occasions to compete against other world-class athletes to hone their skills in high-pressure environments like the Olympics. Because they know they have relatively few opportunities to compete at this level each year, they don't take any of them for granted, even though they may not draw multitudes of spectators. The athletes know that each competition is an important time to improve upon previous performances and move them toward their ultimate Olympic goals, and so they treat these events as valuable opportunities.

When our opportunities are limited, we recognize the stakes are high and so tend to approach each event with more care. Rather than being casual and justifying a cavalier attitude by thinking they don't matter because there will be plenty more chances, we focus intensely and ensure we respond with our best effort to maximize our possibility of success.

Look back over your calendar for the past year. You had a specific number of appointments, each an opportunity to communicate with prospects or deepen relationships with clients. How did you do? How would you rate your attention and effort toward each of these meetings? What score would you give yourself for each of the following?

- Preparation

- Thoroughness

- Listening

- Eye contact

- Empathy

If you had understood a year ago that your meeting opportunities for the coming 12 months were going to be limited, what would you have done differently to hone your skills and improve your performances to move you closer to successfully achieving your business goals?

Your meetings are limited opportunities, period. When you become used to holding many meetings, you may start to take them for granted. While there will likely be chances for more meetings in the future, the danger is in unwittingly adopting a blasé attitude that leads to settling for inferior performances. When you don't consistently perform your best, you communicate to prospects and clients that they are not very important to you. You would probably be offended and angry if your surgeon, pilot, or attorney treated you this way. You hold an important element of people's lives in your hands because you manage a significant source of their financial security. They expect—and deserve—your best; if they don't consistently receive it, they are likely to look for another advisor. If you don't treat every opportunity as a chance to perform exceptionally, sloppy behavior will creep in. It might start with being a little too casual about meetings with smaller clients, or not being as thoroughly prepared as possible for prospect consultations.

Let's say you land a meeting that holds the greatest opportunity you've had for a long time. If these people sign on they'll become your largest client. You're excited, hoping that everything will go well. The prospects arrive and you begin the meeting, sensing things are going well as they listen to you describe how you help people. They've been listening for a while, so you assume they're interested in what you're saying. You explain your views on investing, saving, and the markets in general. You describe your process and what they can expect as clients. Yet, halfway through your presentation you start feeling like you're not connecting with them.

You feel like you're a step behind and start sensing your prospects may be looking for someone a little more seasoned than you. They've asked you a few questions, but the tone of these questions is clearly shifting. Insightful, spontaneous conversation ends, and they start giving clipped answers to your questions. Things are feeling awkward. You try to drive the meeting to more positive ground, but it's going nowhere.

As the wife glances at her watch for the third time in several minutes, you begin considering how to wind down the meeting as graciously as possible. Knowing you can't ask for their business, you ask them if they have any more questions and finish the meeting as quickly as you can. You walk back into your office frustrated and disappointed. You close your door feeling deflated, knowing you won't be hearing from this couple again.

What exactly went wrong? The following story will provide some clues.

MEETING POSTMORTEM

Maria and I had recently started working together when she began our week's coaching call by telling me about a prospect meeting she'd had with Anthony and Tania the day before. She had met Anthony at a networking function and had anticipated he and his wife would likely become clients. Maria's tone told me it had not gone so well, even before she got all the words out.

"I could've done better. I know I could've done *way* better," she told me. "I got lazy…well, maybe not lazy, but complacent. I didn't realize it until it was too late. I'm kicking myself now. You and I spoke about poise less than a month ago, and that's what I want to be showing in every meeting. It sure didn't happen this time, though."

When we walked through the meeting step-by-step from prep to close, Maria began seeing clearly what she could have done differently (and what she planned to change before her next prospect meeting the following day). While some less-than-perfect aspects of the meeting might have seemed inconsequential in and of themselves, when clustered together Maria realized how she had not practically, mentally, or physically prepared as fully as she could have. We listed the steps she had taken, and then alongside each item we worked through what the ideal approach or action would look like so she knew what to focus on next time. (See Figure 10.1.)

Problem: Not Sufficiently Rested

Maria complained she didn't feel sharp during the meeting. When I pressed why, she admitted time had gotten away from her the night before, and she had been up later than she intended.

Solution

The start of a great meeting happens at least a day before you sit down with your prospects or clients. Adequate rest is foundational to high-quality focus. Because you have a finite number of meetings each year, you want to make every one of them count. Treat each meeting as an opportunity to perform your best. You give yourself the best chance for success when you deliberately turn in early the night before so you can be rested and alert. Be disciplined, anticipating any potential distractions such as a friend calling and wanting to catch up, responding to Facebook posts, or watching another episode of a favorite TV show. These activities aren't bad things to do the night before a meeting, but set a definite time to turn everything off and unwind to get ready for sleep, anticipating your great opportunity the next day.

Premeeting Prep	What Maria Did	Best Practices
5+ days prior		• Book meeting room.
3 days prior		• Create written meeting agenda.
2 days prior		• Review agenda and email to prospect/client. • Email direction and parking details.
Day Before		• Print, bind all documents ready for presentation. • Prepare documents to sign. • Review final documents to confirm all is complete. • Check any AV/computer system to be used during presentation. • Confirm meeting room availability.
Night Before		• Mentally rehearse meeting process, including practicing specific questions and dialogue. • Review cues you'll use to ensure you're remaining attentive. • Tidy office in case prospect/client ends up there. • Check refreshments and clean dishes for tomorrow.
	• Stayed up late.	• Get to bed at a time to allow for good rest.
Meeting Day	• First time checking meeting room availability. • Reviewed documents just before meeting start. • No time for routine because finalizing documents.	• Check meeting room is tidy and ready. • Ensure refreshments are ready. • Block out time for your premeeting routine (walk, quiet time alone, music, visualization, etc.). • Pause and take a deep breath before going to greet prospects/clients.
During the Meeting	• Started meeting under stress and distracted by last-minute rush. • Unfocused during conversation. • Defensive/closed body language because of fatigue. • No specific call to action, weak wind-down.	• Confidently, warmly, and calmly greet prospects/clients. • Ask preplanned ice breaker questions to set the tone for the meeting. • Ask open-ended questions and use other good conversation techniques. • Deliberately bring focus into the meeting room. • Heed pre-determined cues to ensure you are keeping engaged and fully listening. • Be mindful of your body language. • Be clear about your call to action, next steps, and timing. • Advise when you'll follow-up.

Postmeeting		• Send email, including:
		  · Thank-you for meeting
		  · Summary of action steps and timing
		  · When you will follow up
		• Follow through on what you said you'd do.

Figure 10.1 Maria's Meeting Postmortem

Problem: Meeting Space Issues

Maria said she panicked when she got into the office that morning and saw someone else had signed up to use the conference room at the time of her meeting. She said she meant to check it the day before but forgot when she got busy.

Solution

When you share a meeting room, always make sure you check the details of your booking early the previous day. This way, if someone has already booked the space, you won't be caught unaware with little time to spare, or worse in front of your client or prospect. The people you're meeting with will primarily take their emotional cues from you, and if you start a meeting flustered and anxious, they'll likely feel uncomfortable, too. When you realize there is a conflict over the room booking well before your meeting, you still have time to make other arrangements. The next best venue option is likely to be your office (which is a good motivator to keep your office tidy). If that's not possible for some reason, have a go-to, last-resort meeting spot planned. I had a client who occasionally met her clients at a coffee shop. She had established a relationship with the coffee shop owner and would let him know in advance when she and clients would meet there. He kept a quiet table at the back open for them at the appropriate time. She had arranged for the owner to bring them coffee when they arrived, and she settled the bill with him later after her clients were gone. Have your own Plan B and even a Plan C meeting space option to turn to if you suddenly need it.

Be sure you email your prospects clear, written directions to your office or other meeting place. Have directions to your office posted on your website. If parking can be problematic, let them know ahead of time where to park. If they need to park in a paid garage, remind them to bring their ticket so you can validate it. Know maximum parking time limits around your office building so you can remind them of these to ensure they won't be facing the unpleasant prospect of a parking ticket after their time with you.

If you plan to offer coffee, tea, or water, make sure you have clean cups and glasses, fresh milk, and sugar. Make time before your meeting to ensure you have what you need or have time to go out and get it.

Problem: Missing Documents

Maria said shortly before the meeting, as she was looking through the documents she was going to present, she realized a page was missing from her Introduction Folder.

Solution

Just like you confirm the meeting room in advance, compile and check all your presentation materials at least one day *before* a meeting. You'll see if anything is missing and have time to write, print, or copy whatever is needed. Any printer or copier problems won't be the source of a last-minute scramble because you can download content to a flash drive or even email it to a copy center near you to print what you need there.

If you're using a computer during your presentation, make sure it's functioning properly before the meeting. Ensure it's plugged in or has a full battery and the program is operating as expected. Check that the screen is clean and bright so your prospect will be able to see it clearly. If you use any slides, keep them to a minimum and mainly visual, with graphs or pictures rather than lots of words to read. Know exactly when you will use them during your presentation. Your objective isn't to impress people with your materials, technology, or presentation skills. You want to have a conversation so you get to know your prospects better and can determine if they will be a good fit among your select number of clients. Take care of the details beforehand so you are free to shine, focused on communicating how you help people and earning your prospects' trust. Be professional and be ready.

Problem: Off Your Routine

Normally Maria would take a short, brisk walk before a meeting. She liked to get some fresh air and focus on the upcoming meeting, arriving back at her office 20 minutes before the scheduled meeting time. This time, she had skipped her normal routine because she was scurrying to complete her Introduction Folder.

Solution

Stick to your own premeeting routine. Take deliberate, thoughtful actions that help you focus and give you the greatest chance to maximize your upcoming opportunity. Some advisors go for a walk and listen to music, some close their office door to get a few moments of quiet, others read something motivating they keep specifically for times like this. You can visualize your meeting, picturing exactly what you want to happen and seeing yourself relaxed, alert, and responsive. Imagine yourself listening attentively and answering clearly. Hear your assured, precise, positive tone. Sense the energy level in the room and imagine directing the tempo and content of the dialogue to suit the situation. See your client or prospect relieved and thrilled with what you're proposing. By having a preset routine, you're sending a signal to yourself that it's "game time"—time to perform at your best. You confidently know you're prepared to take a great next step toward your goal.

Problem: Rushing and Reacting

Because of her haste to put together presentation materials and having skipped her usual premeeting routine to help her get focused, Maria's adrenaline was driving her. She felt rushed when she entered the meeting room. She had not mentally scripted the meeting flow she was hoping to experience and didn't specifically plan her opening words. She also reflected that she had interrupted and completed some of Tania's sentences, instead of letting her finish speaking.

Solution

As we covered in Chapter 5, having a mental script and rehearsing what you will say is not disingenuous or contrived. It *is* a way to be well prepared to make a great impression by succinctly communicating important information. It also allows you to be a better listener because you already know where the conversation is headed.

Often at prospect meetings you and the people you're meeting with are strangers. Anticipate that both they and you will be a little nervous to begin with. Being nervous is normal—those butterflies just mean you care about what's about to happen. These feelings can help keep you alert so you perform at your best. (Anxiety and fear are different—they're problems that typically arise from not being adequately prepared for what is about to happen.) Knowing what you want to say will help you relax. Then, the sooner you can put others at ease, the more likely they'll be to open up to you.

As we discussed earlier in this book, use open-ended questions to facilitate discovery. Closed-ended questions are fine when you're doing a fact finder, seeking information like educational background or address details, but at opening stages of a meeting these questions can make it difficult to get to know a person and usually make the meeting feel more transactional than relational. At initial meetings, you want people to share their perspectives on money, savings, and investments. You want to find out about personal relationships, financial dreams, goals, and concerns. What things are on their mind? What keeps them up at night? What gets them up in the morning? What financial successes have they had? How did they see their parents handle money? Show you are listening and engaged by modeling their answers and asking for further details, saying things like, "It sounds like having sufficient funds for your children's education is really important; tell me some more about why this concerns you right now."

Letting others finish speaking can be a tough conversational skill to master. While it's natural to want to show someone you're tracking with what they are saying, resist the urge to jump in and finish their sentences, even if you are agreeing with what they are saying. Do not ever interrupt a client or prospect.

If something unexpected does force you to divert your attention shortly in advance of a meeting, stop a moment before you greet your prospects to take a couple of deep breaths, relax your shoulders, and smile. Know that the situation that came up will still be there when you complete your meeting, but this immediate opportunity with this prospect might never happen again. Focus on what's immediately in front of you. Rely on your prepared plan and script. Mentally let go of the things outside the meeting room, take your time, and eagerly anticipate learning about your possible next long-term, great, and compliant client.

As you develop your service process with clients, you will want to provide an agenda for your meetings, including important items you intend to cover during your time together. Email it to them a day or two in advance. Let them know you're looking forward to their review and ask them if there is anything not listed they specifically wish to cover. Your agenda will get your client focused on your meeting, let them know you're prepared, and help you clearly and effectively direct the course of the conversation.

Problem: Losing Focus

Maria felt she had not done a good job using nonverbal ways to connect with her prospects. Between Anthony and Tania, Anthony took the lead in the conversation. Toward the end of the meeting Maria realized she had been much more focused on Anthony and had not been making as much eye contact as she should have with Tania. Also, as the meeting wound down Maria felt her fatigue catching up with her and found herself slouching and sitting with her arms folded.

Solution

Maria recognized that she could improve in these more subtle, yet compelling ways to make personal connections. Body language is often an effective way to communicate about what you're thinking and how you're feeling, sometimes more powerfully than through words alone. Maria understood that maintaining eye contact with people shows you're actively listening and eager to hear what they have to say. Women are just as likely as men to control the finances in a relationship, so it is critical to include both partners in a conversation about finances. When meeting with more than one person, share eye contact among all at the table. This might take a bit of practice so it does not feel awkward, but it will help you be more engaging and make everyone feel like they're an important part of the conversation. (If this doesn't come naturally, practice direct eye contact when talking with family and friends to make this feel more comfortable.)

Posture and body language are also important in communicating interest in and openness to what others are saying. Crossed arms and legs imply defensiveness or rejection of what another person is saying. Crossing your arms places a barrier between you and your prospect or client. Practice what to do with your hands and feet so you feel relaxed and natural in open-body positions. If standing, keep your hands at your sides and both feet flat on the floor. If seated, rest your hands in your lap or on the table and keep your legs uncrossed as you sit upright or even lean forward in your chair, which will keep you alert and help communicate attention and interest in what others are saying.[1]

Problem: A Weak Finish

Finally, Maria said she felt she finished the meeting weakly: she let things just wind down and didn't end with a specific call to action.

Solution

Don't let your meetings end abruptly or in a haphazard way. Planning the end of your meetings is as important as planning your openings. Just as building a habitual routine for how you begin your meetings, having a preplanned process for closing a meeting is essential to a successful outcome. Develop a method you're comfortable with, practice saying it out loud, and use it regardless of the size of assets your prospect might have. Your closing will leave the final impression on their minds, so be clear, brief, and specific about what next steps would look like. Because confused minds never buy, lead your prospects so that there is no ambiguity about what their next choices or decisions are. Your closing conversation might go like this: "Before I mention what next steps would look like if we do work together, do you have any questions about what we've covered so far?"

Answer any questions they have, and when there's nothing else they want to know you can say something like: "The next steps to begin working together would have us dialoguing further about your specific goals and objectives, discussing details about your investing comfort levels, and completing some account opening paperwork. Then, once you're on board, we'll finalize formulating and implementing your investments. We'll keep you informed of how everything is moving along while your money is transferred through to our side. Then, once it's arrived, we'll talk again, ensure you're satisfied with how we're allocating everything, and go from there."

While they might not begin working with you, it won't be because they didn't understand how to respond next. Though first impressions certainly count, final impressions set the stage for success.

BRINGING YOUR BEST

Maria said she wanted to show more poise in her meetings. Poise is "a dignified, self-confident manner or bearing; composure; steadiness."[2] Some people refer to it as "being in the zone." Poise is the result of a prepared mind. Getting in the zone comes from practicing and following a routine. You anticipate what will happen next and have time to respond to it with grace and calm assurance. Sometimes you see poise during a sporting event when certain athletes are playing so well that it seems like everyone else is moving in slow motion. They seem to be able to anticipate what's going to happen moments before it unfolds and respond flawlessly. Whether you are an advisor or an athlete, poise sees you through the swirl of activity and distractions surrounding you. Poise enables you to focus so you can hear your own thoughts above the din and see what needs to happen next.

Poise allows you to be your best, every time. Approaching meetings unprepared, thinking you will just "wing it" or get by with your "B game" is foolish and will cost you. The idea of a B game is really just an excuse for a subpar approach when you know you can deliver better; it's an attempt to justify laziness and sloppiness. There is either your best effort or mediocrity. You won't hit everything perfectly every day, but that doesn't mean you should not prepare.

If you enter an appointment knowing you're going to give a B effort, you get a failing grade before you even begin. Even if you land the deal, you still don't get a passing grade because it means you don't respect your client enough to *believe* they deserve your best effort. If you throttle back your focus and attention to detail based on how much you think it will take to secure the business, you'll build bad habits, and bad habits will end up costing you when you can least afford it. You'll lose business that you should have won.

Any repeated action ingrains habits. Bringing and being your best at every opportunity will initially require extra effort, thinking, and consideration, but you'll soon build good habits into your meeting routine. You may not win every prospect you meet with, but it won't be because you weren't performing your best. Remember: Consistent performance is a way to earn the *right* to expect success.

DISTRACTION-PROOF STEPS

- Be best prepared.

- Know your process—and stick to it.

- Communicate clearly.

Regardless of how many meetings you have each year, your opportunities to connect with prospects and clients are finite. Make the most of each event with good planning and preparation, which starts well before prospects walk in your door. Successful meetings aren't a matter of chance—they're a matter of connecting with people. Bring your best every time, build outstanding habits, and earn the right to expect success from every meeting.

EPILOGUE
NOW WHAT?

"Time is going to pass, regardless of what you do with it.
A year from now, it will feel a lot better to look in the rearview
mirror and see 12 months of actions that are moving you toward
your goal, than to still be where you are today, looking at the map,
and considering what path to take. So, get going!"

– PAUL KINGSMAN, SPEAKER, AUTHOR,
EXECUTIVE COACH, AND OLYMPIC MEDALIST

Remaining focused and following a process isn't easy, but it works. Remember where we started: succeeding in this business is simple, but it's not easy. Successful people from any field will tell you their most notable achievements have much more to do with consistently doing the small things well than discovering complicated or secret processes.

If followed, the process we've covered in this book should have you being wildly successful:

- Clarify your picture of why you're building this business.

- Set TARGET Goals, so you know specifically where you are going and when you plan to arrive.

- Choose the investments, services, and types of clients that fit you.

- Plan and practice what you need to say.

- Stay on track with the business choices you've made.

- Recognize how and why you get distracted and take precautions so distractions don't derail you.

- Use systems and practices to keep you focused on getting the important things done.

A lot of people don't like to say it (or hear it), but the reality is success takes effort. But, it is definitely worth it when you reach your goals and enjoy the benefits of what you have worked for. Getting started is key; plan well, but then move beyond the planning and start taking action. Use the tools and techniques listed in this book to enhance your business. Take advantage of help offered (such as downloading the templates and other resources from www.DPAresources.com). As you start making changes and experience positive results, come back to the principles in this book and see what you can fine-tune to help you enjoy that success you want sooner.

GETTING ANOTHER VIEW

Building a business can be lonely at times, and it can be difficult to see where you should concentrate your efforts to effectively accelerate and improve what you're doing. Getting another perspective can be invaluable.

Minimizing drag is vital to swimmers, for whom mere split-seconds separate champions and simply good competitors. When I was training for the Olympics, my coach would often videotape me underwater so we could analyze what was going on beneath the surface and identify drag points I could not see or feel myself. With his help I was able to make slight changes to correct weaknesses in my stroke that were slowing me down or vulnerabilities like sloppy turning techniques that could cost me in the future. I could have done all types of strength and fitness work, but any benefit of that work would still be hampered by unseen inefficiencies in the water. I needed another perspective to identify and eliminate the drag. In the end, this type of consistent attention to the small details made the difference in my swimming career: only four one-hundredths of a second separated me from fourth place and missing a spot on the Olympic medal dais.

Working with a coach in your business can help you see previously unnoticed unproductive habits and inefficient approaches that are slowing you down. A good coach who understands this industry will have seen many advisors' businesses and can bring fresh ideas gained from his or her broad vantage point. A coach can also provide accountability when you face the difficult work of breaking old habits that have to go before you can effectively take on new routines and best practices.

SETTING NEW GOALS

The process in this book is repeatable. Once you have reached your initial goals, like an athlete, you'll face decisions about what to do next. Honestly and thoroughly review what worked and what you would like to change going forward. Congratulate yourself for your successes and identify areas to improve further. Consider how quickly time has gone by and realize the coming months will go just as quickly. Consider the reasons why you are doing what you do and update them, if necessary. Set new goals and put them in the TARGET Goal format to give you measurable and time-bound objectives so you can continue to enjoy the fruits of your focus, determination, and diligent daily practice.

As a coach to advisors, please let me know how I can help you toward the business you want. Visit PaulKingsman.com/coaching to learn more and to contact me so we can set a time to talk about your objectives and how you'll achieve the great success you dream of.

Stay distraction-proof, keep focused, and remain clear about the business you're building—one where you'll gain control, work smarter, and succeed sooner.

HELPFUL RESOURCES ONLINE

Throughout the book, I have suggested you visit www.DPAresources.com to access blank templates and other resources to use in your own planning processes for your business and for more information about methods I've recommended. Following is a list of the material referenced in this book that will be available when you log in to www.DPAresources.com. You may even find a few more useful bits on the site when you visit. You will need to enter your name and email address to access this material. I hope to "see" you online.

From the Introduction

- "Study Reveals Financial Advisers are Not Completely in 'Control' of Their Time and Businesses," Financial Planning Association Research & Practice Institute Report media release

- *Doing More With Less: A report on time management and adviser productivity,* the full report from the Financial Planning Association Research & Practice Institute about advisors not feeling in control of their time or businesses

From Chapter 2

- Further instructions about TARGET Goals

- Blank TARGET Goal templates

From Chapter 8

- Further instructions about how to use the Distraction-Proof Pathway format to clarify the benefits of reaching your TARGET

Goals and to identify specific actions you will take to reach those goals

- A blank Distraction-Proof Pathway template

- Further information about time-blocking and examples for planning your own week

- A blank weekly calendar to create your own time-blocked days

ACKNOWLEDGMENTS

I thought writing a book would be infinitely easier than winning an Olympic medal—no swimsuit, no chlorine; just sit, think, and type. Now, at the end of this project, if you asked me which was easier to accomplish, I'd say grab your swimsuit! Like the team of backers whose efforts were vital to getting me on that Olympic dais, there is a team of people who I am indebted to for their help in creating this book in your hands. God has blessed me by bringing great, wonderful, kind, and patient people into my life who have helped me enormously.

To Hilton Brown, my swimming coach for 15 years, thanks for keeping me motivated and teaching me to focus on what matters most. To Nort Thornton, my swimming coach at UC Berkeley, thank you for continually challenging me to look at things differently, even though I thought I already knew everything. I am grateful to you both for your insights, which profoundly shaped my perspective and ultimately influenced this book.

Thank you to Vicki and Paul Gray who have been constant boosters for 30 years. Vicki, I will always be grateful to you for introducing me to this great industry; you helped me begin this journey and have been there as a mentor every step of the way.

To Doug Evans, Jim Wagner, and Carl Lundgren: if we're judged by the caliber of company we keep, I rest easy. Your constant support, prayers, accountability, and humor made completing this book easier. I thank God and you for your love and faithfulness.

Thank you to John Eggen at Mission Publishing for your writing and publishing program, which provided the framework and accountability to get my thoughts into ink. Thanks to my writing coach, Jill Cheeks, for your encouraging enthusiasm and helpful insights that helped shape this book.

To David Russell, Stephen Wershing, Donna Skeels-Cygan, Laurie Itkin, and Neville Ann Kelly, all published authors: thanks for your availability and for sharing information to help shorten my journey. Special thanks to Dave for generously sharing your TARGET Goal concept.

To Cynthia Zigmund, my publishing consultant: thank you for your guidance, wisdom, and insights to fine-tune this book and your great help to push it across the finish line. Thank you also to Summer Morris for giving this book a visual personality and to Jack Kiburz for helping me choose the best words and mind my p's and q's.

To my coaching clients: thanks for the opportunities to have input into your businesses. You constantly keep me developing better ways to communicate how to remain distraction-proof in the midst of this exciting and demanding business.

To Kirk Ludwig, Matt Taddei, Diane McCracken, and my colleagues at TLA Financial: thank you for the freedom and patience you've shown while I have brought this project to completion.

To Maree (Mum) and Dennis (Dad) Kingsman and Linda Kolodzinski (my sis): thank you for your wisdom in "training me up." Everything I am is thanks to you and your love and guidance, which provided the foundation for my life. No one could ask for a more encouraging family.

Finally, to my wonderful wife, Aliesha, and remarkable son, Jack: What a team! Thanks for...well, everything. Aliesha, God gave me a helpmate like no other in you. Jack, your tech expertise astounds me and your humor brings me joy. This book and my speaking would be impossible without the help, patience, and inspiration you both give me. Thank you both for loving me so dearly!

NOTES

Introduction

1. Marketdata Enterprises Inc., "The U.S. Weight Loss Market: 2014 Status Report & Forecast," https://www.bharatbook.com/healthcare-market-research-reports-467678/the-us-weight-loss-market-2014-status-report-forecast.html (accessed June 20, 2014).

2. Financial Planning Association, "Research and Practice Institute>2014 Time Management and Productivity Study," http://www.onefpa.org/business-success/ResearchandPracticeInstitute/Pages/2014-Time-Management-and-Productivity-Study.aspx (accessed April 17, 2014).

Chapter 2

1. David Russell, "Goals That Work," In Success With People (Barnabas Smyth Publishing, 2005), 157–58.

Chapter 4

1. Duncan McPherson and David Miller, "Client Classification and Triple-A— An Ideal Client Profile," In Breakthrough Business Development (Mississauga, Ontario: John Wiley & Sons, Canada, Ltd., 2007), 43–47.

Chapter 8

1. David Rock, *Your Brain at Work* (New York: HarperCollins Publishers, 2009), 51–59.

2. Kathie F. Nunley, "Keeping Pace with Today's Quick Brains," Dr. Kathie Nunley's Layered Curriculum Web Site for Educators, http://help4teachers.com/ras.htm (accessed November 1, 2014).

3. M.T. Gailliot, R.F. Baumeister, C.N. DeWall, J.K. Maner, E.A. Plant, D.M. Tice, L.E Brewer, and B.J. Schmeichel, "Self-control relies on glucose as a limited energy source: willpower is more than a metaphor," *Journal of Personality and Social Psychology* 92, no. 2 (2007): 325–36.

4.   Financial Planning Association, "Research and Practice Institute>2014 Time Management and Productivity Study," http://www.onefpa.org/business-success/ResearchandPracticeInstitute/Pages/2014-Time-Management-and-Productivity-Study.aspx (accessed April 17, 2014).

5.   Ibid.

6.   John Medina, *Brain Rules* (Seattle, WA: Pear Press, 2008), 87.

7.   Eyal Ophir, Clifford Nass, and Anthony D. Wagner, "Cognitive control in media multitaskers," *Proceedings of the National Academy of Sciences* 106, no. 37 (2009): 15583–15587.

8.   Clifford Nass, "The Myth of Multitasking," interview by Ira Flatow, *Talk of the Nation*, NPR, May 10, 2013.

9.   "Interview: Clifford Nass," *Frontline Digital Nation*, PBS, February 2, 2010.

10. Ibid.

Chapter 10

1.   Craig W. Lemoine, "Communicating Effectively with Clients," In *Financial Planning: Process and Environment*, 5th ed. (Bryn Mawr, PA: American College Press, 2013), 2.25–2.28.

2.   *Dictionary.com*, s.v. "poise," http://dictionary.reference.com/browse/poise?s=t (accessed November 15, 2014).

INDEX

ABOUT THE AUTHOR

Paul Kingsman is a sought-after expert on how to be distraction-proof. He teaches financial services professionals how to maintain focus to successfully grow their businesses and achieve outstanding long-term results.

He knows the importance of keeping focused in life's split seconds first-hand: he trained for 13 years to swim a two-minute backstroke race at the Olympics and won a medal by only *four one-hundredths* of a second!

As an Olympic medalist, Paul knows the principles and processes needed to succeed in a highly competitive environment. As a financial advisor, he understands the daily business realities of this industry. His experience enables him to equip audiences and coaching clients with practical solutions to overcome distractions, pursue their priorities, and increase their AUM.

After completing his studies at the University of California at Berkeley and retiring from competitive swimming, Paul applied the same success habits he had developed in the sport to business, going on to achieve big results with companies such as Speedo and Morgan Stanley, both in his native country of New Zealand and in the United States. He has worked on the retail side of the financial services business with a wire house, bank, and RIA, as well as on the wholesale side with an asset management firm, giving him a broad understanding of the challenges advisors face.

With clients such as Wells Fargo, New York Life, AIG SunAmerica, BlackRock, Bank of America, and UBS Financial Services, Paul has helped advisors at some of the world's most prominent financial companies to gain control, work smarter, and succeed sooner.

Paul has a Master of Theological Studies from Golden Gate Baptist Theological Seminary and is a chaplain at Marin County Jail. He and his wife live in the San Francisco Bay Area and enjoy hanging out and laughing with their adult son. For more information about Paul, his speaking, and his coaching, visit www.PaulKingsman.com.

HAVE PAUL KINGSMAN SPEAK AT YOUR NEXT EVENT

WWW.PAULKINGSMAN.COM

Paul Kingsman speaks to financial services professionals at regional and national sales meetings, sponsored events, and professional conferences.

Combining his background as a financial advisor and his experiences as an Olympic medalist, Paul understands advisors' challenges and how to focus amid countless distractions. He brings fresh perspectives and practical solutions, showing advisors how to achieve their key goals and objectives sooner.

Audiences quickly recognize Paul speaks their language. In his presentations he details issues advisors face daily and equips them with mindsets, actions, and words that work. Advisors leave highly focused, better prepared, and more confident to turn prospects into clients and clients into loyal advocates.

Paul's engaging and applicable programs are available as keynotes, breakouts, and workshop sessions.

To learn more or book Paul Kingsman for
your upcoming event, visit www.PaulKingsman.com.

Made in the USA
Monee, IL
29 June 2020